The Land and People of

VENEZUELA

PORTRAITS OF THE NATIONS

The Land and People of®
VENEZUELA

by *Geoffrey Fox*

HarperCollins*Publishers*

Country maps by Philip Stickler/Stickler Cartography

Every effort has been made to locate the copyright holders of
all copyrighted materials and to secure the necessary permission
to reproduce them. In the event of any questions arising as to
their use, the publisher will be glad to make necessary changes
in future printings and editions.

The map on page 18 is adapted from *Venezuela: The Search for Order,
the Dream of Progress* by John V. Lombardi. Copyright © 1982 by Oxford
University Press, Inc. Used by permission.

The maps on pages 33, 69, 84 are adapted from *Latin American History:
A Teaching Atlas* by Catherine J. Lombardi and John V. Lombardi, with
K. Lynn Stoner. Copyright © 1984 by The University of Wisconsin Press.
Used by permission.

THE LAND AND PEOPLE OF
is a registered trademark of
HarperCollins Publishers.

For information address HarperCollins Children's Books, a division of
HarperCollins Publishers, 10 East 53rd Street, New York, NY 10022

Library of Congress Cataloging-in-Publication Data
Fox, Geoffrey.
    The land and people of Venezuela / by Geoffrey Fox.
        p.   cm. — (Portraits of the nations)
    Includes bibliographical references (p.   ) and index.
    Includes discography: p.
    Summary: Introduces the history, geography, people, culture,
government, and economy of Venezuela.
    ISBN 0-06-022476-2. — ISBN 0-06-022477-0 (lib. bdg.)
    1. Venezuela—Juvenile literature. [1. Venezuela.] I. Title
II. Series
F2308.5.F69 1991   90-20431
987—dc20   CIP
                                                        AC

1 2 3 4 5 6 7 8 9 10
First Edition

To
MY PARENTS,
who started me on my way,

Y a los amigos y desconocidos,
criollos y musiúes,
que me enseñaron
a querer a Venezuela.

Contents

THE WORLD

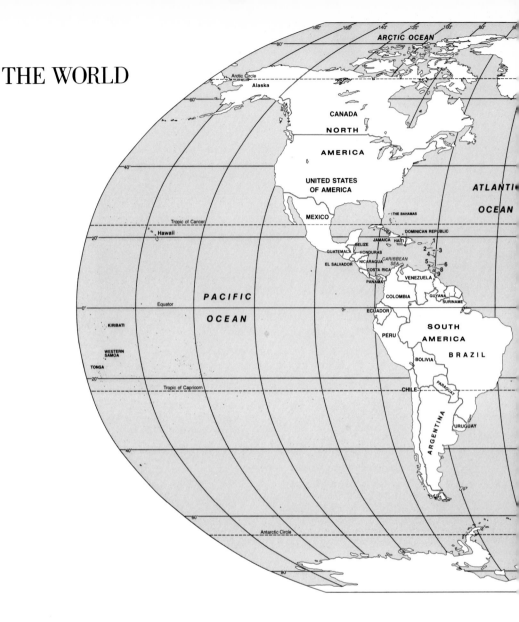

This world map is based on a projection developed by Arthur H. Robinson. The shape of each country and its size, relative to other countries, are more accurately expressed here than in previous maps. The map also gives equal importance to all of the continents, instead of placing North America at the center of the world. *Used by permission of the Foreign Policy Association.*

Legend

—————— International boundaries

------------ Disputed or undefined boundaries

Projection: Robinson

0	1000	2000	3000 Miles
0	1000	2000	3000 Kilometers

Caribbean Nations

1. Anguilla
2. St. Christopher and Nevis
3. Antigua and Barbuda
4. Dominica
5. St. Lucia
6. Barbados
7. St. Vincent
8. Grenada
9. Trinidad and Tobago

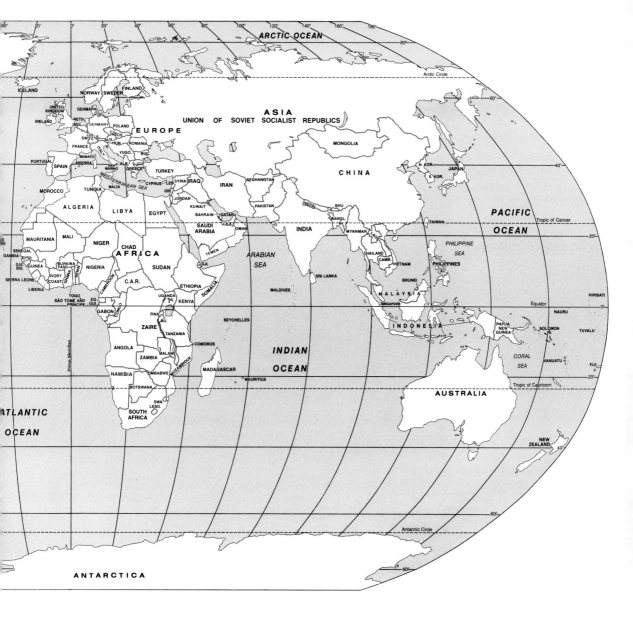

Abbreviations

ALB.	—Albania	C.A.R.	—Central African Republic	LEB.	—Lebanon	SWA.	—Swaziland
AUS.	—Austria	CZECH.	—Czechoslovakia	LESO.	—Lesotho	SWITZ.	—Switzerland
BANGL.	—Bangladesh	DJI.	—Djibouti	LIE.	—Liechtenstein	U.A.E.	—United Arab Emirates
BEL.	—Belgium	EQ. GUI.	—Equatorial Guinea	LUX.	—Luxemburg	YUGO.	—Yugoslavia
BHU.	—Bhutan	GER.	—Germany	NETH.	—Netherlands		
BU.	—Burundi	GUI. BIS.	—Guinea Bissau	N. KOR.	—North Korea		
BUL.	—Bulgaria	HUN.	—Hungary	RWA.	—Rwanda		
CAMB.	—Cambodia	ISR.	—Israel	S. KOR.	—South Korea		

Mini Facts

OFFICIAL NAME: Republic of Venezuela (República de Venezuela)

LOCATION: Northernmost country in South America, facing the Caribbean Sea on the north and the Atlantic Ocean on the northeast; Colombia borders the country on the west, Brazil on the south, and Guyana (formerly British Guiana) on the east.

AREA: 352,143 square miles (911,698 square kilometers)

CAPITAL: Caracas

POPULATION: 19,246,000 (1989 estimate)

MAJOR LANGUAGE: Spanish

RELIGION: Roman Catholic; minority of Protestants and very small minorities of non-Christian religions

TYPE OF GOVERNMENT: Constitutional democracy

HEAD OF STATE: President

HEAD OF GOVERNMENT: President

LEGISLATURE: Bicameral

LOCAL DIVISIONS: 20 states, 2 federal territories, federal district, federal dependency

ADULT LITERACY: 88 percent

LIFE EXPECTANCY: Male, 65 years; female, 70.6 years

ANNUAL PER-CAPITA INCOME: $2,629 (1985)

MAIN PRODUCTS: Oil (5th-largest producer) and oil products; steel; coffee; fruits

Introduction

Venezuela is a land of beautiful beaches, tropical jungle, snow-capped mountains, and the highest waterfall in the world, with wild creatures from ocelots to crocodiles, toucans to purple ibis, and wild plants and flowers of every color and size.

Perched on the northern edge of South America, facing the North Atlantic Ocean and the Caribbean Sea, it has been a favorite landing spot for raiders, traders, and pirates for hundreds, perhaps thousands, of years.

Its coast was the first place Christopher Columbus landed in South America, and the first European settlement on the continent was founded there. Three hundred years later, Venezuela was the first colony in Latin America to declare independence from Spain.

Venezuela is the homeland of many heroes of the struggle for independence, including the Liberator, Simón Bolívar, and was the site of some of that conflict's most vicious battles.

National Symbols, Official and Unofficial

Venezuela's most important national symbol is the Liberator, Simón Bolívar, whose statue is found in every city. The national flower is the orchid, of which more than five hundred varieties grow in the country. The national tree is the yellow-blossomed *araguaney*, which grows in almost all parts of the country. The national bird is the *turpial*, yellow with black bands on its back. It is often kept as a pet for its singing voice.

The *pabellón nacional* (national flag), first raised by Francisco Miranda in 1806, consists of horizontal bars of equal width, yellow, blue, and red, with an arc of seven stars for the original seven provinces that declared independence in 1810. There is also a meal that is so symbolic of Venezuela it is called *pabellón criollo* (local folks' banner). It is a plate of shredded beef, white rice, black beans, and slices of fried plantain, which each cook prepares in her or his special way.

The national anthem is a popular song from 1810, with fierce but stilted lyrics from the war for independence. Its chorus is: "Glory to the brave people / who threw off the yoke, / respectful of law, / virtue, and honor," and the first verse begins: "Down with chains! / cried the Lord; / and the poor man in his hut / asked for Liberty."

Many Venezuelans prefer a much gentler, lyrical song that is sometimes called "the second national anthem": *"Alma Llanera"* ("Soul of the Plains"). Traditionally played on a rustic harp, it has verses describing the banks of "the vibrating Arauca river," herons, roses, palm trees, and the "carnations of passion" of Venezuela's great plains.

Beach in Cata Bay, Aragua State.   Vladimir Sersa

It is blessed with fertile soil and ample mineral wealth, from iron ore and bauxite to diamonds, gold, and jasper. But its greatest prosperity has come from exporting products to satisfy some of the world's great cravings: first chocolate, then coffee, then petroleum, and now television.

And the strategy has worked well, especially in this century. In a few decades, Venezuela went from being an overwhelmingly rural society to being mainly urban—88 percent of its 19 million people live in towns of over 20,000 inhabitants, roughly a third of them in four cities. It has achieved one of the highest literacy rates in Latin America. And despite

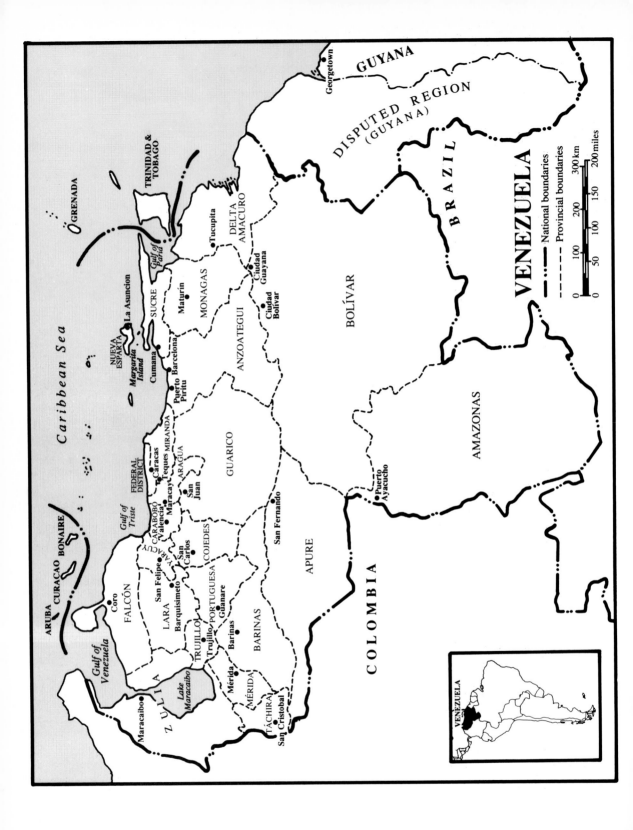

serious economic problems in the last few years, it is still the country with the highest per-capita income in all of Latin America.

After a long and difficult period of race conflict, civil wars, and dictatorship, it is one of the most racially harmonious countries in South America, and it has had the continent's longest period of constitutional democracy.

Indian houses like these, known as palafitos, *on stilts in the shallow waters of Lake Maracaibo, inspired early European explorers to call the area "Venezuela"—meaning "Little Venice."* Graziano Gasparini

Presidents of Venezuela

Note: Many Venezuelans use the mother's family name (surname) after the father's, but still consider the father's surname to be the important one. In this list, to avoid confusion, the main (father's) surname is written in capital letters.

José Antonio PÁEZ	1830
José María VARGAS	1835
Carlos SOUBLETTE	1837
José Antonio PÁEZ	1839
Carlos SOUBLETTE	1843
José Tadeo MONAGAS	1847
José Gregorio MONAGAS	1851
José Tadeo MONAGAS	1856
Julián CASTRO	1858
Pedro GUAL	1859
Manuel Felipe TOVAR	1860
Pedro GUAL	1861
José Antonio PÁEZ	1861
Juan Crisóstomo FALCÓN	1863
José Ruperto MONAGAS	1868
Antonio GUZMÁN Blanco	1870

This "Allegory of Progress" from the 1880's is full of symbols of patriotism and modernity. The president at the time, Antonio Guzmán Blanco, is shown next to a portrait of Venezuela's most revered hero, the Liberator, Simón Bolívar. The seven stars, under the arm of the female figure representing "Progress," stand for the seven original Venezuelan provinces that declared independence from Spain. In the center is the national shield, with three more symbols: in the upper left, a sheaf of wheat with seven stalks for those same provinces; in the upper right, victory is represented by crossed weapons and banners bound by a laurel wreath; in the bottom, a galloping white horse. Collection of the Venezuelan National Library

Francisco LINARES Alcántara	1877
Gregorio CEDEÑO	1878
Antonio GUZMÁN Blanco	1879
Joaquín CRESPO	1884
Antonio GUZMÁN Blanco	1886
Juan Pablo ROJAS Paúl	1888
Raimundo ANDUEZA Palacio	1890
Guillermo Tell PULIDO	1892
Joaquín CRESPO	1892
Ignacio ANDRADE	1898
Cipriano CASTRO	1899
Juan Vicente GÓMEZ	1908
Victorino MÁRQUEZ Bustillos	1915
Juan Vicente GÓMEZ	1922
Juan Bautista PÉREZ	1929
Juan Vicente GÓMEZ	1931
Eleazar LÓPEZ Contreras	1935
Isaías MEDINA Angarita	1941
Rómulo BETANCOURT	1945
Rómulo GALLEGOS	1948
Military *Junta*	1948
Governing *Junta*	1950
Marcos PÉREZ Jiménez	1952
Governing *Junta*	1958
Rómulo BETANCOURT	1959
Raúl LEONI	1964
Rafael CALDERA	1969
Carlos Andrés PÉREZ	1974
Luis HERRERA Campins	1979
Jaime LUSINCHI	1984
Carlos Andrés PÉREZ	1989

The Venezuelan flag flies over a ferryboat to the island of Margarita. Rafael Salvatore

The Land

The Setting

Venezuela is the fourth-largest country in South America (after Brazil, Argentina, and Colombia). Covering 352,143 square miles (911,698 square kilometers), it is more than twice as big as California, and bigger than France, Spain, and Portugal together. Venezuela's neighbor to the west is Colombia, to the south Brazil, and to the east Guyana (formerly the colony of British Guiana). To the north is the Caribbean Sea, and to the northeast, the Atlantic Ocean.

Venezuela is very close to the equator, the part of the earth that never tilts away from the sun. For this reason, temperatures stay pretty much the same year round. In the highest mountains of the country, the peaks are freezing and permanently covered with snow; in the lowest areas, the air is always hot, often over 100°F (38°C), especially in places that get little wind. In the hills and high valleys of the north and northwest, where most of the people live, the air stays around 70°F (21°C) year round.

Much of the Gran Sabana looks today just as it did when the Europeans first arrived.
Margot Hernández

It is a land of extreme contrasts, not just in temperature but also in the type of rock and soil, the amounts of water, and the kinds of plants and animals that can survive in one area or another. There are thousands of distinct little zones, each with its own climate and ecosystem.

These zones can be grouped into five major regions: the Coastal Lowlands, around the northern and eastern edges of the country; the Andes Mountains, the country's highest, rising in the west; the Coastal Ranges, two parallel chains of mountains separated by high, lush valleys, stretching across the northern part of the country; the Llanos, wide plains south of the Coastal Ranges; and the Guiana Highlands, which Venezuelans call the Guayana, the southeastern section that makes up almost half the country and contains dense jungle and strange and ancient rock formations.

Tropical Rainfall

What Venezuelans call "winter"—*invierno* in Spanish—is the rainy season, which lasts from May through November in most parts of the country. The dry season is called "summer"—*verano*. In the Llanos and the state of Amazonas, 60 to 80 inches (150 to 200 centimeters) or more fall each year—which is a lot, especially since almost all of it falls in a few weeks in the early part of "winter." Caracas gets around 33 inches (90 centimeters) a year, about as much as Chicago.

Tropical rains are very impressive. The sky seems suddenly to open up and dump enormous quantities of warm water. The water crashes through the palm branches and onto roofs and roadways

How the Land Was Made

About 3 billion years ago, before there was a continent of South America, some of the molten lava at the core of the earth began to cool into huge clumps of igneous rocks (from the Latin word for "fire"). This became what geologists call the "basement" underneath all of South America, beneath layers of soil and mountains, such as the Andes, that were formed much later.

In the Guiana Highlands of southeastern Venezuela, this ancient rock—some of the oldest in the world—rises above the surface in massive, nearly perpendicular, flat-topped mountains, which the Indians called *tepuis*. In all these billions of years, rainfall and the many crisscrossing rivers have eroded the softer parts of the rock, leaving the *tepuis* isolated like gigantic monuments. From one of these the world's highest waterfall, Angel Falls, drops 3,212 feet (979 meters)—fifteen

with so much noise that people can't make themselves heard, and as they huddle in doorways or hop through puddles, they have to gesture to make themselves understood. On the slopes around the cities, covered with thousands of shacks, the dirt paths become slippery channels of mud, and every so often part of a hillside gives way, carrying some of the shacks crashing down onto the homes below.

The rain may let up a bit, then increase again, and then—just as suddenly as it began—it stops, sometimes after twenty minutes, sometimes after an hour or more. The sun comes out, and in the countryside men pull off their shirts to squeeze them dry and women try to wring out their skirts, and people resume whatever they were doing before the rain.

times higher than Niagara Falls. The great heat and pressure that went into creating the *tepuis* also formed the diamonds for which this region is famous.

The continents were (and still are) slowly, slowly floating on huge "plates" above the molten core of the earth. About 130 million years ago, in the Cretaceous period—when dinosaurs were still roaming the earth—South America separated from North America, and some time after that it broke off from Africa. It remained isolated from all the other continents for millions of years, and the animals and plants there evolved independently, producing species that existed nowhere else. Many are now extinct—for example, a sloth that was nearly twenty feet long. But other odd creatures, then unknown in other parts of the world, still survive. They include smaller sloths, armadillos, tree-dwelling anteaters, and opossum rats.

Then, about 15 million years ago, the shifting plates under North

Some Forest and River Creatures of Venezuela

Tapirs and monkeys, though relative newcomers, have thrived in Venezuela. So have numerous rodents, including some very odd ones. The capybaras are the largest rodents in the world. They are just like giant guinea pigs, up to four feet long and weighing up to 160 pounds (72 kilograms)—much too big for most people to keep as pets, but people who have eaten them say they're delicious roasted.

Tapirs don't make good pets, either. They grow to 400 pounds (180 kilograms) and have bulky, rounded bodies and snouts like

The chigüire, as the Venezuelans call the capybara, is the largest rodent on earth.   Gabriel Gaszó

miniature elephant trunks, which they hold above the water when they're swimming. On land, they are as graceful on their slender legs as deer.

As for the monkeys, one study has found over sixty-four species in Central and South America, many in Venezuela. They are unrelated to those in Africa and Asia, and are the only monkeys in the world that can hang by their tails. The Indians catch and tame many kinds as pets. The capuchin monkeys, which are very clever and can be trained to do tricks, are the favorites; these are also the ones used by organ grinders. The howler monkey, one of the largest species, is not tamed but hunted for food. It makes a roar like a series of drum booms that can be heard a mile away.

Armadillos come in dozens of varieties in Venezuela—one kind can weigh as much as 100 pounds (45 kilograms). Called *cachicamos* in Venezuela, these armor-plated creatures with pointed snouts are treated with affection and are the heroes of many Venezuelan folktales, along with the giant tortoises, called *morrocoys*. *"Cachicamo diciéndole a morrocoy conchudo"* means "Armadillo calling the tortoise shelly," something like "the pot calling the kettle black."

Another shelly creature is the caiman. Unlike their cousins, the alligators, caimans have bony overlapping scales on their bellies, perhaps to protect them from the razor-toothed piranhas, or caribe fish, that live in the same rivers. When the German naturalist Alexander von Humboldt explored Venezuela in 1800, there were huge swarms of caimans on the Orinoco River, some 20 to 24 feet (6 to 8 meters) long. Most caimans are between five and seven feet. The biggest ones have almost disappeared, hunted almost to extinction for their hides.

The Orinoco region is also home to anacondas, the largest snakes in the world—the record was one 37.5 feet (11 meters) long. They coil up in the trees, waiting to drop down onto some tasty animal or person, but they are also excellent swimmers and can attack from the water of the Orinoco and other rivers. They can squeeze a grown caiman to death. Boas, which are usually under ten feet long, are more friendly; some families keep them in the house to hunt rats. Only one kind of rattlesnake made the trip from North to South America (the United States and Mexico have about twenty-five species), but it is especially deadly. There are also electric eels that can stun a horse.

Among the strangest of all the creatures in the Orinoco are freshwater dolphins. Humboldt was amazed when he found a school of these aquatic creatures, close cousins of those that live in the ocean, 1,200 miles (1,900 kilometers) inland from the mouth of the Orinoco. There are also freshwater manatees, mammals that usually live in the ocean. They nurse their pups from two teats on the chest and have sometimes been taken for mermaids. These are among the signs that the basin of the Orinoco and Amazon rivers was once part of the sea.

America and South America collided, pushing up the rock that formed Central America. Along this land bridge armadillos, opossums, and other animals from South America gradually worked their way north, and animals from North America, such as bats, deer, tapirs, bears, otters, monkeys, dogs, and cats, spread south.

At about the same time that North and South America became joined, there was another collision. The Nazca Plate, under much of the Pacific Ocean, and the South American plate crashed together, forcing the rock upward along the whole western coast of South America, forming the Andes mountains. These two plates are still pressing against each other, and when one or the other slips just a little, the pressure is released in earthquakes. Although not as frequent as in the Andean countries farther south, such as Chile and Peru, where the pressure is greatest, devastating earthquakes do occur in Venezuela from time to time.

Between the Guiana Highlands in the southeast and the Andes in the west and northwest of Venezuela, a wide strip of lower land gradually filled with sedimentation, bits of rock worn down from the mountains and carried by the rains and rivers. This is how the Llanos (Great Plains) of Venezuela were formed.

The Coast

Venezuela's 1,750-mile (2,820-kilometer) coastline, running mostly east–west, has several good harbors and two large gulfs, the Gulf of Paria in the east, between Venezuela and Trinidad, and the Gulf of Venezuela in the northwest.

The coastal lowland is only a few miles wide for most of the distance. Behind it lies a wall of mountains, broken only by a valley around Puerto Píritu. The coastland is mostly very dry and hot, with some beautiful sandy beaches around Puerto La Cruz and Cumaná, east of La Guaira, and around Puerto Cabello. The area around Paraguaná Peninsula in the west, partly framing the Gulf of Venezuela, is very, very dry—desert movies have been filmed on its dunes.

Around the western and southern edges of the Gulf of Venezuela and all around Lake Maracaibo, in the northwest corner of Venezuela, the land is low, flat, and soggy. A sticky black substance used to ooze out of the ground, sticking to the Indians' sandals and the explorers' boots. The Indians called it *mene* and used it to patch their huts and canoes.

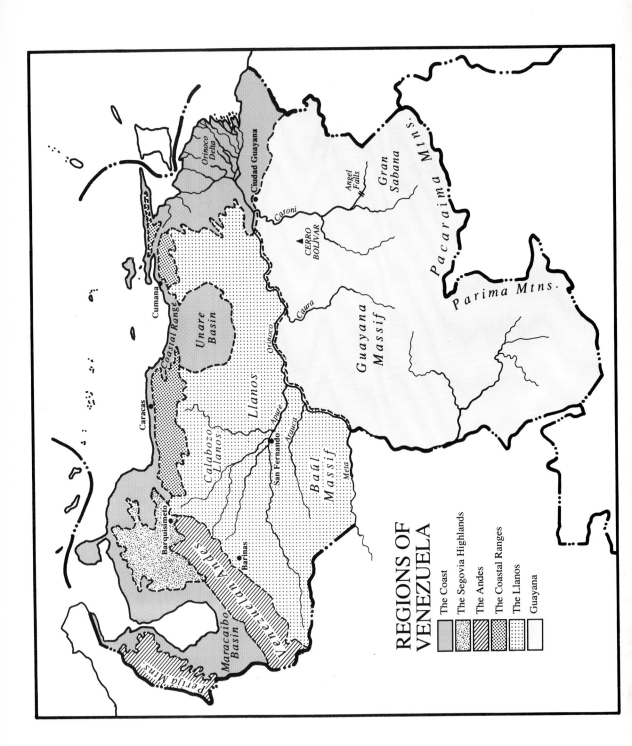

REGIONS OF
VENEZUELA

- The Coast
- The Segovia Highlands
- The Andes
- The Coastal Ranges
- The Llanos
- Guayana

Today people pump it out of the ground and use it for energy, and call it "petroleum." Oil wells are a common sight in the lake and on its shores, the natural gas burning like a torch at the top of the latticework day and night. Because of the oil, the city of Maracaibo, at the entrance to Lake Maracaibo, has grown to be the second-largest city in the country.

The Coastal Ranges and Their Valleys

Sailing along the northern coast from east to west, the way Alonso Ojeda and Amerigo Vespucci did in the first Spanish reconnoiter in 1499, one sees a wall of mountains rising above the palm trees, just a few miles inland from the beaches. The mountains rise from behind Cumaná and continue for about 36 miles (58 kilometers) to the west. Then—after passing the lowlands around Puerto Píritu—the ship will pass by another, higher wall of mountains, also rising just a few miles beyond the beach, and extending from Cape Codera to Golfo Triste (Sad Gulf) in the west.

This mountain wall discouraged Ojeda and would slow down exploration of the central region for years. Later, the mountain wall would protect the towns in the valleys behind them from pirate raids.

South of this range is the country's most fertile and populous area, a string of valleys that are 30 miles (48 kilometers) across at the widest places. It is in this band that agriculture, transportation, and communications have always been most developed. The Indians here were growing corn, pineapple, potatoes, yucca, and many other plants before the Europeans arrived. Today most of the cities and towns are in these valleys, including Caracas, the capital.

Approaching Caracas from the north, sea captains and airplane pilots can aim toward the Pico (Spanish for "peak") Avila, 7,081 feet (2,159 meters) high, the highest in the area. Caracas lies in the valley just the

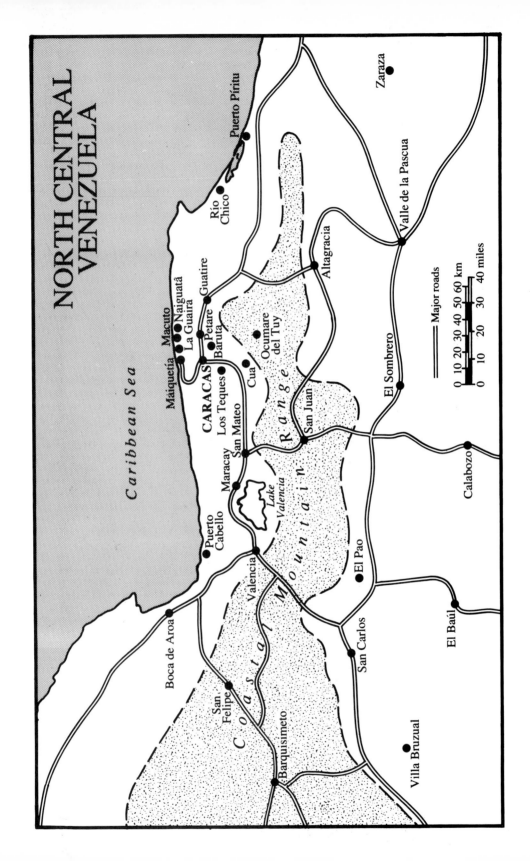

NORTH CENTRAL VENEZUELA

Caribbean Sea

Zaraza

Puerto Píritu

Valle de la Pascua

Río Chico

Altagracia

Guatire

Macuto

Naiguatá

La Guaira

Petare

Baruta

Ocumare del Tuy

El Sombrero

Maiquetía

CARACAS

Cua

Los Teques

San Mateo

San Juan

Maracay

Calabozo

Lake Valencia

Puerto Cabello

El Pao

El Baúl

Valencia

San Carlos

Boca de Aroa

San Felipe

Villa Bruzual

Barquisimeto

Coastal Mountain Range

Major roads

0 10 20 30 40 50 60 km

0   10   20   30   40 miles

other side of it. In 1895, when New York society journalist Richard Harding Davis took an offbeat pleasure trip to Venezuela, the fastest way to get from the seaport at La Guaira to Caracas was by a train that wound its way over the mountain. In *Three Gringos in Venezuela and Central America* (1896), he wrote that "its tracks cling to the perpendicular surface of the mountain like the tiny tendrils of a vine on a stone-wall, and the trains creep and crawl along the edge of its precipices, or twist themselves into the shape of a horseshoe magnet, so that the engineer on the locomotive can look directly across a bottomless chasm into the windows of the last car."

The modern road is much straighter and shorter, tunneling through the mountains. Davis and his companions were relieved to find that Caracas, at a little more than 3,000 feet (900 meters) of elevation, is about 10°F (6°C) cooler than La Guaira (which is at sea level). Caracas temperatures range from a high of about 70°F (21°C) in July down to 66°F (19°C) in mid-January.

Beyond the northern valleys is a second, lower chain of mountains, the Inner Range. Here the highest peaks are less than 5,000 feet (1,500 meters), and the whole range gets lower as it goes east. It ends at the Unare River, 50 miles (80 kilometers) farther east than Cape Codera. When the Europeans arrived, people were growing corn and tobacco on these slopes, crops that were completely new to the Europeans.

There are more high hills along the coast still farther east, ending at the ridges on the peninsula of Paria. This peninsula reaches out into the Caribbean toward the island of Trinidad (once part of Venezuela, but now an independent country).

The Andes

In the western part of the country are the Venezuelan Andes, much higher than the mountains along the coast. These are a continuation of

View of the town of Apartaderos, in the Andes, at 10,500 feet (3,200 meters) above sea level.   Graziano Gasparini

the Andes that run parallel to the whole Pacific coast of South America. They turn northeast to enter Venezuela, where they divide into two sections. One, the Perijá range, heads north along the Colombian border. The other, beginning south of Lake Maracaibo and running northeast, is known as the Cordillera de Mérida, also known as the Venezuelan Andes. The highest points in the country are all in this

Frailejones *(a kind of plant) on the snowy heights of the Pico del Aguila (Eagle Peak, or Beak), Mérida State.*   Vladimir Sersa

cordillera (Spanish for mountain range). Several peaks reach 7,000 to 9,000 feet (2,100 to 2,700 meters). Pico Bolívar, the highest, rises 16,427 feet (5,007 meters) above sea level, Humboldt is 16,214 feet (4,942 meters), and Bompland 16,040 feet (4,889 meters). The city of Mérida lies in a valley 5,380 feet (1,636 meters) high, and is surrounded by these spectacular peaks. The air is thin, cool, and clear up in these mountains and in the high valleys, where many little towns nestle. Since the middle of the nineteenth century, this has been the main coffee-producing region of the country.

The Segovia Highlands is a transitional area of low mountains between the Andes and the Coastal Ranges.

Isolated in a region with a unique climate and soil conditions, the people here have developed a culture and way of speaking which is quite distinctive from that of other parts of Venezuela. They are known for their rather formal speech and for the heavy wool *ruanas*, square blankets with a hole for the head, worn by men and women alike—the side usually worn on the outside is dark blue, the other bright red. The Andes have also been a base for political power. For almost sixty years, from 1899 to 1958, men from the Andean state of Táchira, near the Colombian border, dominated the nation as military dictators. The current, democratically elected president, Carlos Andrés Pérez, is also from Táchira.

Llanos and the Orinoco Delta   South of the inner range
of mountains lie the wide, grassy plains known as the Llanos, home of the *llaneros* (plainsmen). The Llanos stretch across the country for nearly 1,000 miles (1,600 kilometers), and their widest point is 200 miles (320 kilometers), from the mountains of the north to the banks of the Orinoco River in the south.

The Llanos were ideal country for the grass-eating cattle, horses, and donkeys that the Spaniards first brought over from Europe in the 1600's. Alejo Carpentier, a twentieth-century Cuban writer who lived for several years in Venezuela, called the Llanos "The Land of the Horse," because almost all human activity, whether for work or play, was performed on horseback, and everything else depended on horse transportation, or had to do with caring for horses. Cavalry chiefs from the Llanos ruled Venezuela in the early years of the republic, from 1830 to about 1880.

The Llanos are subject to extreme changes from the wet to the dry season. In "winter," from May until the end of November, the rains swell the rivers by as much as twenty or thirty feet, flooding wide areas. Early explorers sometimes mistook these flooded plains for inland seas.

Guri Dam near Puerto Ordaz, Bolívar State. Vladimir Sersa

Sir Robert Schomburgk, a German explorer working for England, described such a sudden rise of water on the Rupununi River in 1843, when he and his companions

saw the flood at a distance of a mile or two come rushing over the savannahs. We shall never forget that sight; there was something peculiar in seeing so great a mass of water, which threatened us with imminent danger. . . . The expanse of water resembled an extensive lake. The snow-white Egrette [egret] in great numbers, the American stork, the stately Jabiru, cormorants, and large flocks of spurwing plovers, enlivened the surface above, while the tops of trees, granite blocks clothed in tropical vegetation, and here and there a small spot of elevated ground, alone remained visible.

Then, when the rains stop, the plains dry out so thoroughly that the ground cracks open and animals die of thirst. Most of the rivers turn to dry gulches. The larger rivers, such as the Meta, the Apure, and the Caroni, still carry water, though, and all of these flow into the Orinoco.

The Orinoco and Its Delta

The Orinoco flows for 1,600 miles (2,500 kilometers), entirely inside Venezuela. It begins in the far south of the country, in the territory called Amazonas, and traces a wide curve, like the letter C. It starts out going northwest, then north, then, for its longest and widest stretch, northeast. Near the top of the C it is joined from the west by another large river, the Meta, and a little farther north by the Apure from the northwest. East of Ciudad Bolívar, the Caroni comes up from the south and also joins the flow of the Orinoco.

Finally, the Orinoco breaks into hundreds of smaller streams fanning out and flowing into the Atlantic Ocean. This is the Delta Amacuro, a land of twisting, intersecting rivers and streams and small islands, dense vegetation, and hundreds of species of birds, monkeys, snakes, caimans, fish, and insects.

All these tributaries, and many smaller ones, make the Orinoco the second-largest river in South America. The only one bigger is the Amazon, farther south in Brazil. In 1800, the German naturalist Alexander von Humboldt confirmed the amazing fact that the Orinoco and the Amazon are connected. The Casiquiare "canal"—actually a small river—flows southwest from the Orinoco into the Río Negro, which then flows into the Amazon, making this "the only natural waterway in the world connecting two giant river systems," as Douglas Botting, who retraced Humboldt's steps, describes it. Some of the thickest jungle in South America is in the area between these two great rivers.

Sir Walter Ralegh (also spelled Raleigh), one of the first European explorers in this area, entered on a channel called Manamo from the Gulf of Paria in the north, between Trinidad and Venezuela, in 1595. He and his crew had to row hard against the current, but when they reached the Orinoco and turned southwest, they were able to use their sails. This is because the prevailing winds are from the east. Ralegh was so impressed by the size of the river, he thought one could sail west on it all the way to Peru. But Indians and fevers kept him and his men from going farther than a point near modern Ciudad Bolívar.

Later, merchant vessels and warships would enter the Orinoco through one of the eastern channels, such as the Boca Grande (Large Mouth). This allowed them to use their sails almost all the way. When they were ready to return, the sailors furled the sails and let the current carry their boats back to the Atlantic. This combination of winds and current turned the Orinoco into a major highway for European explorers, settlers, and merchants, so the area bordering the Orinoco was one of the earliest developed regions of the country.

During the rainy season, which in this region usually lasts from April to December, the Orinoco is so wide and deep that ships of 1,500 tons (1,360 metric tons) can enter from the Atlantic and steam all the way to Puerto Ayacucho, a distance of 1,035 miles (1,670 kilometers). Larger ships must stop about 250 miles (400 kilometers) inland, where huge black slabs of stone rise in the river and make it too narrow for them to proceed. Here, in 1764, almost two hundred years after Ralegh's trip, the Spaniards founded the town of Angostura, which means "narrows." (Angostura bitters, which used to be sold as a cold remedy and is now used as a flavoring in cocktails, is made from the bark of a tree from this area.) It was a major center for the conquest and settlement of the interior of Venezuela. Its modern name is Ciudad Bolívar.

The Orinoco and its tributaries have been major transportation routes and food sources throughout history. In recent times the power of the Caroni has been harnessed by the huge Guri Dam, just south of Ciudad Guayana, to produce electricity.

The Guayana

The Orinoco is the boundary between the Llanos and the southern highlands that were formed when the continent was made. The name for this region, from a Carib Indian word, is spelled in different ways in different countries—Guyana, Guiane, Guiana. In Venezuela, it is called the Guayana. It includes the spectacular high plains called the Gran Sabana (Great Savannah) and the heavily forested southern region called Amazonas territory.

From Ciudad Bolívar today, little single-engine planes fly over the dense tropical forests south of the Orinoco. After about an hour, the plane comes suddenly upon Auyán Tepui (the devil's mountain), rising nearly 8,400 feet (2,600 meters) through the mist. It is a dark, broad-based, concave, flat-topped cone, roughly symmetrical except for a gaping canyon. If this is a tourist flight, the little plane heads straight into that maw, past white waterfalls gushing from the rock face at each jagged turn. Then it reaches its objective. From the very top of the *tepui*, a pair of thick, flickering ribbons of water, immense volumes of water, plunges into the mist. This is Angel Falls, the highest in the world. The plane dips its wingtips slightly left, then right, in the twin torrents, giving everyone aboard a good look. Then rivers, a lagoon, more falls, and jungle come into view, and the plane drops gently to a clearing.

Auyán Tepui covers more than 270 square miles (700 square kilometers) in the northwest quadrant of Venezuela's Canaima National Park, the sixth-largest national park in the world. It contains 11,583 square miles (30,000 square kilometers) of jungle, savannah, and *tepuis*, abruptly rising mesas isolated by millennia of erosion. The conjunctions of these dissimilar terrains, intersected by rivers that rise as much as 30 feet (9 meters) in the rainy season, create innumerable microclimates for the astounding variety of fauna and flora. This terribly complex environment is also terribly fragile, depending on intricate balances among the many living elements.

The Great Savannah and the rain forest come together around the *tepuis*. The Venezuelan savannah is an immensely broad, flat land covered mostly with high grasses, with clumps of forest around the many rivers and streams. The soil does not retain as much water in the dry season as in parts of the Llanos, leaving too little grass for cattle raising. This, and the remoteness of the area, are the main reasons it remains sparsely populated. The flatness of the savannah makes the *tepuis* look even more dramatic.

The air here is rich with oxygen and the fragrances of fruits and flowers. The colors of birds and flowers are startlingly brilliant. Howler monkeys, birds, insects, and other creatures make the air alive with sound, especially in Amazonas.

It is easy to understand why such novelists as W. H. Hudson, Arthur Conan Doyle, Alejo Carpentier, and Rómulo Gallegos all imagined protagonists getting lost or going mad in the Guayana. Such earlier explorers as Sir Walter Ralegh and Alexander von Humboldt were awestruck by the power of nature and the many strange animals and plants.

Embedded in the ancient stone are diamonds, gold, iron, and other minerals, including semiprecious red- and gold-colored jasper glittering through waterfalls near Roraima—a huge *tepui* on the southeastern border with Guyana and Brazil.

Wild pineapples, orchids and moriche palms are among the many plants growing here. When Ralegh saw a pineapple, he called it "the princesse of fruits that grow under the Sun." When his ruler, King James, first tasted one, he proclaimed it "a fruit too delicious for a subject to taste of."

This ecosystem is now threatened by developers and treasure hunters. Diamond and gold prospectors, hydraulic engineers, missionaries, and tourist developers have all made their marks on the forest and savannah, some of them ugly scars. And now there is a newer threat.

Auyán Tepui, one of the great ancient rock formations of the Guayana region.   Gabriel Gaszó

Measuring Angel Falls

Known to the Pemóns as Churún-merú (falls of the river Churún), Angel Falls were discovered for the outside world in 1935 by an American bush pilot, Jimmy Angel, who was looking for gold. He insisted, from altimeter readings, that they were a mile high.

Two years later, still hoping for gold, Angel landed on top of Auyán Tepui and got stuck—he, his wife, and two other companions had to abandon the plane and managed to hike back to civilization. The plane remained there until the Venezuelan Air Force dismantled it in 1970 and flew the parts away by helicopter. Today it sits in a hangar at the Ciudad Bolívar airport.

It wasn't until 1949 that a party led by the American journalist Ruth Robertson reached the base of the falls to measure them accurately—2,648 feet (805 meters) in the first main drop and 3,212 feet (976 meters) to the river at the very bottom, making them the highest in the world. Still, it was well short of a mile, and Jimmy Angel was sorely disappointed.

On the Robertson expedition, the Pemón porters were very reluctant to approach what they called a "devil mountain," and took the precaution of painting their faces red to guard against the *canaimas* (*canaima* is the Pemón word for "evil spirit").

Around and even inside the park, and farther south in Amazonas territory, *garimpeiros*, prospectors from Brazil, have been laying waste wide swaths of forest and poisoning the waters at a furious pace. While the 3-billion-year-old *tepuis* will probably remain erect, their fragile biosystems may soon feel the effects of altered rainfall patterns and species losses.

Venezuela's Dispute With Guyana

Venezuelan maps show a large area to the east labeled "Disputed Territory." It looks like a fat tail on Venezuela. This area was once part of the Spanish Empire, and Venezuelans think they should have inherited it. It was taken in the 1800's by the British, who kept moving their guardposts farther west while Venezuelans were too busy fighting civil wars to do anything about them.

An international arbitration panel set the present boundary in 1899, but Venezuela has challenged that decision, claiming that Britain had illegally occupied the region. The amount of land claimed by Venezuela is immense: 61,400 square miles (159,000 square kilometers), roughly five eighths of the territory of Guyana, running all the way to the Essequibo river, which splits Guyana down the middle. It is sparsely populated, and so far its resources have not been heavily exploited.

Whatever the merits of Venezuela's legal arguments, it is inconceivable that Guyana would surrender so much of its territory peacefully; discussions between the two governments have gotten nowhere. The great potential wealth of the Essequibo region, in petroleum, timber, and minerals, and the likelihood of increasing population pressure in Venezuela, could lead to a more serious and less pacific conflict. Although for now a military invasion seems unlikely, Venezuela has built up its army installations near the border.

For now, most of the park remains almost as wild and awesome as when Sir Walter Ralegh stumbled through here in 1595 looking for

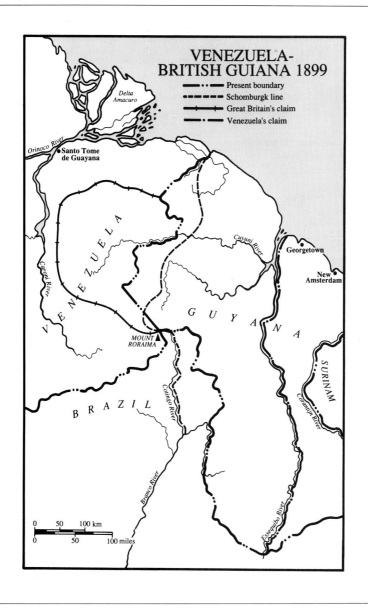

VENEZUELA-
BRITISH GUIANA 1899

Present boundary
Schomburgk line
Great Britain's claim
Venezuela's claim

"the Great and Golden City of Manoa (which the Spaniards call El Dorado)."

The People

Population Today

In Venezuela there are copper-colored people with green eyes and blond curly hair, chocolate-colored people with sharp-bridged noses and straight black hair, light-skinned people with flattish noses and tightly coiled hair, and every other possible combination of colors, hair textures, face shapes, and bone structures. There are even some people who look entirely European, or African, or American Indian.

Visitors are often struck by the beauty of these people. With such variety, the reason for this impression can't be a particular physical type. What makes so many Venezuelans attractive must be a certain grace of movement, the easy, flowing gestures, the quick broad smiles— cultural traits that convey alertness and warmth. Also remarkable is the

Many kinds of faces gather around at an infant's burial in Cumaná.   Rafael Salvatore

All Dancing to the Same Beat

In Lara, south of Barquisimeto, in such towns as Quíbor and Tocuyo, the feast of San Antonio (June 12–14) is celebrated with dances including the *"Seis por Ocho"* ("Six by Eight"), which was originally a dance of the white landowners similar to a French quadrille; the "Jurumungá," based on the dances of the slaves; and the *"Poco a Poco"* ("Little by Little"), derived from a Spanish folkdance. These dances are accompanied by the Tamunango drums, which come from Africa.

fact that so many of them are young. Nearly 40 percent of the more than 19 million Venezuelans are under the age of fourteen.

The Venezuelan census figures do not indicate race, but a widely used estimate is that 20 percent are "white," 9 percent "black," and two percent "Indian." The overwhelming majority, the remaining 69 percent, are *mestizo* (mixed). These, however, are very rough estimates—some people who would look to an outsider like *mestizos* would identify themselves as "white" or, more rarely, "black."

This is a new race, *"Hecho en Venezuela"* ("Made in Venezuela"). And the culture of the people is every bit as mixed as their genes. How this came about is the story of conflicts, accommodations, and finally mutual acceptance by the three original racial groups.

Before the Europeans: Indigenous Peoples

The first to arrive were the people Columbus called "Indians"—because he thought he was in India. They were really members of many different ethnic groups, organized in tribes sharing common ancestries and dialects. In Venezuela there were at least 110 languages and dialects, which belonged to ten unrelated language families or "stocks." The largest and most powerful set of tribes spoke dialects of Carib. There are still people who speak languages from six of these stocks in modern Venezuela.

Anthropologists today believe the pre-European people of America were descendants of people who had migrated, either on foot or by boat, from widely different parts of Asia and perhaps from the southern Pacific, beginning approximately 35,000 years ago. By 1498, when Columbus reached the coast, there were perhaps 350,000 people living in what is today Venezuela, according to one respected set of calculations.

Nowhere in the country were there great cities of stone, as in Honduras, Mexico, and Peru. The largest settled communities were in the central highlands and near the Orinoco, where people grew corn and other foodstuffs. Their domesticated animals included dogs and monkeys, raised for food, and parrots and other birds, kept mostly as pets; they had never seen cattle or horses, pigs or chickens. None of these settlements could have had more than a few thousand people, and most were far smaller.

Most of the groups in other parts of the country did not farm at all, and thus they could not produce enough food for a large population. In general, the men hunted animals such as tapirs and peccaries (which look something like wild boars) and made war, raiding other communities' food supplies. The women provided most of the food by gathering wild grasses and fruits. In some areas, such as the Orinoco Delta, both men and women caught fish.

The arrival of the Europeans was disastrous for the people on the Caribbean coast of Venezuela and along the Orinoco River, where the Spaniards would capture them as slaves and ship them to the island of

Hispaniola (where the Dominican Republic and Haiti are today), to replace those who had already been worked to death there. In the central highlands, the Teques under chief Guaicaipuro and the Caquetíos in Lara and Yaracuy fought hard against the Spaniards until smallpox, to which the Indians had no immunity, struck in 1580, killing as many as two thirds of them.

The Spanish crown seemed to consider the Indians a kind of natural resource that should not be wasted. It tried to protect them from being massacred or worked to death, partly because of pressure from a few humanitarian priests but mostly so they would last longer and produce more. The favorite system was the *encomienda*, a grant that gave the settlers the right to use Indians for labor but also the obligation to care for them. A "mission" was similar to an *encomienda* but was run by the priests or friars, who were supposed to turn the Indians into Christians.

The *encomienda* system lasted until the late 1700's in Venezuela, much longer than in other, more prosperous colonies, where the white landowners could afford to buy black slaves or hire free laborers. But by the 1700's, many of the horses and cattle brought over by the Spaniards had run wild in the Llanos, and runaway Indians had became skilled horseriders and lived by hunting wild cattle. They were part of the pro-independence cavalry that wiped out the missions of the Orinoco—where Indians were practically slaves—in 1817.

Today, most of the Indians have been absorbed into the general population, having intermarried with other groups and living pretty much like everybody else. Many, maybe even most, people in Venezuela have some Indian ancestry and look it. Indian features are especially common in the people of the eastern coast and in the Guayana.

The Indians' techniques for constructing houses out of palm leaves and mud, their food preparations and herbal remedies, and many of

A traveler with Indian features stops on a road in Bolívar State.   Rafael Salvatore

The Yanomami:
Tenuous Survival of a Pre-Hispanic Culture

The indigenous group that has most successfully resisted the influence of white society is the Yanomami, who roam through the jungle of Amazonas, on both sides of the border with Brazil. Of course, some Yanomami have abandoned the old ways and now live like other people in the towns. But the traditional ones are hunters and gatherers. They neither farm nor build permanent houses, and they use very simple tools and weapons.

Yanomami men hunt with bows that are longer than they are (the bows are nearly 7 feet [2 meters] long, the men are rarely over 5.5 feet [1.7 meters] tall). This seems to be something they learned recently from other tribes—a few generations ago, they did all their hunting by running after animals and spearing or clubbing them to death. They didn't catch much then, and even with arrows they still don't. This means that while the men are out hunting and probably having a good time, the women have to provide the main food by gathering palm fruits, nuts, and other wild fruit. When there is nothing left to gather or hunt, the whole community moves on to a new spot in the jungle.

Yanomami children wear nothing at all. Men and women wear a string tied around the waist and decorated with paints made from seeds. A woman, when she dresses up, will tie shells and beads to her string so that they dangle in front of her like an apron. Both sexes insert ornaments—bones, sticks, or feathers—through their noses, lower lips, and earlobes.

Men and women cut their hair all around at about the level of the top of the ears, and men shave the top of the head with a sharpened sliver of bamboo. Painting the body is very important for communicating with other people and with the magic spirits. When a girl first menstruates, she is painted red, placed in a special hut, and given special food—this protects her from evil spirits, and protects the community. If a menstruating woman goes near weapons, for example, she will take their magic away. When a couple goes visiting, they paint themselves all red or with red and white stripes, because red is a good-luck color. To visit someone without painting oneself is considered very impolite.

One aspect of Yanomami culture that has attracted a lot of attention is their way of settling disputes. If a Yanomami man feels offended by another—for example, if the other man has pronounced his private name—he grunts and bends his head forward. The man challenged then clubs his challenger as hard as he can, right on the shaved top of his head, with a heavy branch covered with rough nobs. If the challenger is still standing, he gets his turn to club the other guy, who stands still and waits for the blow. Naturally, they both get a little dizzy, and the tops of the mens' heads are usually lumpy from scars.

To withstand the pain, a dueler prepares himself by having a friend blow a very potent narcotic called *yoppo* up his nose through a bamboo tube. The duel is over when one man can no longer stand to swing his club. If the offense is not so great as to call for head clubbing, the two men take turns pounding one another's chests as hard as possible.

The Yanomami have been the most successful survivors among Venezuela's pre-Columbian peoples—in 1972, estimates of their population ranged from 25,000 to 40,000, far more than for the other groups. Now, however, their numbers are dwindling rapidly. Their survival is threatened by prospectors, who have found gold in the streams where they live and are rapidly destroying their habitat.

Some African Cultural Survivals

In the 1600's, the church encouraged blacks to join *cofradías* (lodges) to worship their chosen saints. In many cases they continued worshiping their old African gods, simply calling them by the names of Catholic saints. The lodges also helped support the families of members who had died, collected money to buy the freedom of slaves, and financed funerals. Around 1800 the white authorities, perhaps feeling threatened by this organizational power, outlawed the lodges in Caracas and seized their property.

The only lodge that has survived to modern times is that of the Most Holy Sacrament of the Altar of San Francisco de Yare, located in a heavily black area in the hills south of Caracas. The lodge

their spiritual beliefs have become a prominent part of the common culture. Only in a few outlying regions have groups fully retained their Indian identity.

The Africans

The first black African slaves were brought to Venezuela in the early 1500's, mainly to work in the copper and gold mines and on plantations of cacao—wherever the Indians were too scarce or too unmanageable.

The Portuguese, who had been importing black slaves to Europe since 1445, controlled most of the slave trade to the colonies. Some slaves taken to Venezuela had already lived in Spain or in other colonies; others were brought directly from Africa. Most had come originally from the Guinea Coast and, farther south, Angola. They belonged to different groups, each with its own language and customs.

organizes an annual festival of Corpus Christi, with dancers disguised as "devils" and "slave masters" with elaborate, horned masks. The dance seems to be a drama about Africa and slavery, although the participants today are carrying on a ritual whose origin they've forgotten. It is a very colorful performance that has become popular with tourists, and the devil masks are displayed in many homes and offices. On the holidays of St. Anthony, in Lara, and St. John, in Carabobo, dancers carry *Tutumecos*, marionettes on sticks that are held up and made to dance to the music.

Just as the Africans borrowed many things from the Indians, the Indians have also borrowed from the blacks. The Goajiros of northwestern Venezuela perform a dance called Chichamayo that is said to be very similar to an elaborate Afro-Venezuelan dance with drums known as *Tambor Redondo*.

In Barlovento, the eastern third of the state of Miranda; around San Francisco de Yare in the southern part of the same state; and in Aragua and several other places along the coast, so many African slaves were imported that even today these areas are mostly black. African drums, rhythms and rituals are most in evidence there.

In other parts of the country, especially in the hills of Lara and Yaracuy to the west of Caracas, Indians and blacks worked shoulder to shoulder in the copper and gold mines for white masters. They learned one another's magic and respected one another's gods.

One Indian practice that the blacks quickly adopted, because it was thought to have special powers, was smoking cigars. Tobacco is an American plant, which was still unknown in Africa or Europe. The fumes were believed to purify the celebrant in a religious ritual. In the Venezuelan countryside and in the poor areas around the cities, it is still common to see men and women smoking cigars or cigarettes with the lighted end inside the mouth—this was originally done so as not to lose any of the smoke's spiritual or physical power. Today cigars are used in fertility and healing rituals in Venezuela.

Blacks and Indians commonly intermarried, or had children together without marriage. The child of an Indian-black union was called a *zambo*.

A black man who was concerned about the fate of his children had a special incentive for marrying an Indian woman: Under colonial law, any child born to an Indian woman was free, regardless of the color of the father, whereas any child born to a black slave woman was a slave.

The intermingling of Indians and blacks occurred in other ways as well. Runaways from both groups fled into the deep woods or into the Llanos, and the *cimarrones*, or runaway slaves, learned how to survive in this land from the Indians. As early as the 1600's, explorers reported finding tribes of black Indians; these may have been *cimarrones* who were living like Indians or who had been adopted by Indian tribes.

The Spaniards

The Spaniards had the greatest cultural impact, because they made the rules by which everybody else had to live. They imposed their language, their laws, their religion—Roman Catholicism—and many of their attitudes.

The Venezuelan cities of Barcelona, Trujillo, Mérida, and Valencia, among others, were named for the settlers' hometowns in widely separated parts of Spain.

In Caracas, Basque families formed much of the colonial elite, and Canary Islanders were the white working class. They were considered as second-class Spaniards, with less prestige than *peninsulares*, those who had come from the Iberian Peninsula. One of the wealthiest Basque

Spanish traditions survive in the music at this festival of Saint Isidro Labrador, in San Rafael de Mucuchies, Mérida. The man in front is playing a cuatro, *a four-string adaptation of a guitar that is used throughout Venezuela.* Vladimir Sersa

families in colonial Caracas was the Bolívars. Betancourt, a name that would become famous in Venezuela in the mid-twentieth century, comes from the Canary Islands.

During their three hundred years of colonial domination of both blacks and Indians, the Spaniards and Creoles—native-born whites—fathered many mixed-breed children, and some of the whites helped their illegitimate, nonwhite children to set up businesses or learn a trade. By the end of the colonial period, there were so many people of mixed race that they vastly outnumbered "pure" members of any of the three original races.

The Spaniards also brought over attitudes that are still widespread in Venezuela. One of these is that manual labor is degrading and should be performed by servants or slaves, not by gentlemen or ladies. Even today, middle-class men in Venezuela are reluctant to shine their own shoes, and most middle-class women consider it important to have at least one servant to cook and take care of the house.

Honor, Shame, and *Machismo*   *Honor* and *vergüenza* (honor and shame, or a sensitivity to the opinions of the community) are central concepts in traditional Spanish culture. They were even more important in the 1500's, when the Spaniards first arrived.

Men, to defend their honor, believe they must always be competing against other men. In medieval Spain, when a knight on horseback had to be ready to take on all comers, this attitude may have made sense. However, it makes it difficult for two or more knights to cooperate. In the 1500's, a *conquistador* like Lope de Aguirre could put an entire military campaign at risk to gain a personal advantage. Even today Venezuelans, and people in other Spanish-speaking countries, find teamwork more difficult than individual accomplishment.

One thing that men compete for is women, and men in Spanish-speaking countries are notorious for their aggressive attempts at seduction. A common strategy for a single woman is to be as seductive as possible, to get the men to compete for her. When she finds the man she wants, she is supposed to be loyal to him the rest of her life—at least, that's the romantic ideal. Men do not generally feel as constrained to be faithful.

In marriage, there is a traditional division of responsibilities: The man is in charge of things outside the house, the woman of things inside. He is supposed to provide for the family economically, and to make all

Weaving a hammock in Aragua de Barcelona, Anzoátegui State.   Rafael Salvatore

the business decisions for the family. She is supposed to take care of housekeeping, cooking, and bringing up the children.

A woman is not powerless in this system—she can exploit a man's sense of shame, reminding him of his duty to look after her or insisting that his honor will be in question if he does not do something she wants. Mature women in particular can take advantage of their image as mothers to command men's respect.

Still, the ultimate authority over family decisions and property is controlled by the male. Popularly called *machismo* (male-ism), this tradition is centuries old and had even been written into law. In 1980, at the urging of a group of women lawyers, the Venezuelan Congress reformed the law to give women more nearly equal rights, making it easier for them to seek divorce and giving them equal rights over family property and child custody.

However, there are still many households where the husband demands absolute obedience from his wife and uses her earnings as though they were all his, sometimes spending them on other women. Wife beating is a common offense, with the man feeling he has the "right" to do whatever he wants to "his" wife.

These attitudes, left over from the days of knights in armor, but without the chivalry, are gradually giving way as women organize themselves in consciousness-raising groups and learn to use the powers that the legal reform has given them.

Other Ingredients

In addition to the original three-race mixture, blacks from Trinidad and other islands of the West Indies—English-speaking, and with religious and other customs different from Venezuelan blacks—came during the nineteenth- and twentieth-century gold rushes in the Guayana and the beginning of the oil boom around Maracaibo in the 1920's. After World

War II, many Italians, Spaniards, and Portuguese arrived, encouraged by the Venezuelan government. Some of them now feel themselves to be Venezuelan, but quite a number do not.

The heaviest immigration—no one knows how heavy, because much of it is illegal—has been from neighboring Colombia, where wages are much lower. Many Cubans came after the Cuban revolution, and they have had a major cultural impact. One of the country's largest business conglomerates, owning both Pepsi-Cola and Coca-Cola distribution rights, a television and radio station, an airline, and much else, is Cuban owned and run. Other, more humble Cubans have brought Afro-Cuban religious practices which have been adopted, at least superficially, by some Venezuelans. Argentines exiled during their country's military dictatorship were also important in Venezuela in the 1970's, but many of them have since returned home.

The mix of these cultures has created a varied, complex, and lively culture. While there are certainly individuals with prejudices, there is very little social discrimination based on color or appearance, and people of all shades identify themselves as "Venezuelan" rather than of a particular race. But this present harmony did not come about without a great national struggle, beginning in colonial days.

From Colony to the First Republic: 1498–1812

First Encounter

On August 8, 1498, four Carib men paddled a canoe into the Gulf of Paria to investigate the clothed, light-skinned, and bearded strangers who had just arrived on three small Spanish caravels. That was how South America discovered Europe. From that day on, the fate of its people would be tied to events across the sea, especially in Europe and, later, North America.

Christopher Columbus, in command of the little fleet, on his third voyage across the Atlantic, thought he had reached the outskirts of the Earthly Paradise. What the Caribs thought of Columbus is not known, but they soon had reason to regret their friendliness. Columbus took some of them captive, and the explorers and conquerors who came after him would be much crueler.

The Early Colony

First Explorations   Right after Columbus, Amerigo Vespucci explored the northern coast from the Orinoco delta to the Gulf of Venezuela, in 1499. His book about the *Mundus Novus (New World),* as he called it, so impressed the German mapmaker Martin Waldseemüller that in 1507 he labeled the new lands "America," from the Latin version (Americus) of Vespucci's first name. Throughout Europe there was great excitement about these discoveries, and the Carib, Warau, Palenque, Caquetío, and other people of the country began to receive many more of these strange, hairy visitors with big ships and steel swords.

The first Spanish settlement in the area was in 1510, on the little island of Cubagua, near the Paria Peninsula, where the Spaniards forced natives to dive for pearls. Because the island is quite dry, fresh water had to be brought from the mainland, where the town of Cumaná

An idealized view of the "Indians of the Guayana," from a book published in Paris in 1763.

The native people were not always pleased to be evangelized. This scene is from a history of "New Andalusia" (eastern Venezuela), published in Spain in 1779.

was settled in 1523. Cubagua is now a ghost town, but Cumaná still exists, the oldest European settlement on the mainland of South America.

On the coast farther west, Coro was founded in 1527. The tall wall of mountains and, especially, the resistance of the native tribes kept the early explorers from going very deeply into the interior, where they hoped to find great cities and riches like those of the Incas in Peru or the Aztecs in Mexico.

But they were disappointed. The Indians of Venezuela had no great cities and very little gold. When Spanish sailors saw a community of huts on stilts in Lake Maracaibo, they called it "Venezuela" (Little Venice—Venecia is the Spanish name for Venice). The only thing this little village of sticks and palm leaves had in common with the famous city in Italy was that the inhabitants went from place to place in boats. This sailors' joke became the name for the whole region.

Oddly, the first governor of the Spanish colony of Venezuela was a German, Ambrosius Alfinger, who took charge of the settlement at Coro in 1529. He worked for the House of Welser, a German trading company specializing in spices and medicinal plants, which had helped finance Charles I of Spain's successful campaign to get himself elected as Charles V of the Holy Roman Empire. In return, Charles granted the Welsers a *capitulación*—what we would call a "concession"—to explore, colonize, and develop Spain's possessions around Lake Maracaibo.

But Alfinger and the other Welser employees spent all their energies looking for El Dorado, the Golden Man. In the process they antagonized the Indians and infuriated the Spanish colonists, whom they ordered around. Most of them came to violent ends. Alfinger was killed by an Indian arrow through the throat in 1531, others starved to death or were killed by Indians or disease, and Philipp von Hutten, the last Captain General (supreme commander) of Venezuela appointed by the Welsers, was beheaded by Spanish settlers in 1541. He was not quite thirty.

The Search for the Magic Kingdom

The Spaniards, Italians, Dutch, Germans, Portuguese, English, and other Europeans who scoured the waterways and forests of the New World believed in many ancient myths and legends, which distorted their perceptions of what they really did see. Christopher Columbus and other navigators of the fifteenth and sixteenth centuries reported seeing mermaids, for example—they expected to see them, because the books they read claimed that they existed. Others claimed to have seen headless men and Amazons.

These stories grew from a combination of Old World and New World

El Dorado

Somewhere in the mountains there was a lagoon, the natives said, where once a year the people covered the body of their naked king with gold dust. They then floated him out into the middle of the lagoon on a raft, with many golden objects that the king would sacrifice by dumping them into the lagoon. This was the person the Spaniards called "El Dorado," the Golden One.

In his *History of New Granada*, completed in 1636, Juan Rodríguez Freyle described this ritual and said it used to take place near Bogotá, today the capital of Colombia. Colombian archeologists have found gold figurines that seem to show a chief on a raft—so maybe there was something to the story. But the Europeans and their Indian informants, getting more excited every time they told the tale, added to it, describing El Dorado as a golden city, somewhere off in the wilderness. The German adventurers who came to Venezuela with the Welser company looked for it throughout the Andes. Sir Walter Ralegh, who insisted the city's real name was Manoa, looked for it on the Orinoco in 1595. Other explorers scouted for it as far away as North America, in what are today New Mexico and Arizona.

The Europeans' gold fever seemed strange to the Indians, who

myths and misinformation. Tales of such marvels as anthills of gold and a fountain of youth somewhere in Asia had been spread by a famous travel book, written about 150 years before Columbus by Sir John Mandeville (nobody knows anything more about him). Even after the European explorers figured out that they were not in Asia, but in some "new" place, they still dreamed of finding these wonders.

generally valued brightly colored feathers, stones, and pieces of silver more highly. Gold was too soft for weapons or tools, and melted at too low a temperature for cookware. But the Europeans had attributed magical powers to gold for thousands of years, telling stories of the Golden Bough from the sacred grove of the goddess Diana, and the Golden Fleece captured by Jason. Gold symbolized all that was noble and pure to them, and European and Arab alchemists had long been obsessed with turning lead into gold. Finally, gold was money—an idea that was incomprehensible to the Indians. If the Europeans wanted it so badly, the Indians were generally quite willing to give them all they had. Unfortunately, they never had enough to satisfy the newcomers.

The gold fever continues. In the 1840's, prospectors rushed to the Gran Sabana, in southeastern Venezuela, when gold was discovered there; and in the 1980's, another rush began in the same region and in Amazonas territory. In the current gold rush, prospectors, many of them crossing illegally from Brazil, have been destroying streams and wildlife with mercury (used in processing the gold), cutting down the fragile vegetation for their airstrips and housing, and killing Indians who get in their way. Near the Venezuelan border with Brazil and Guyana, there is a town called El Dorado.

The headless men were a fairy tale, like the mermaids. Women warriors, however, were real—women as well as men had attacked intruders in the South American jungles with spears and blowguns. But the idea that there was an entire community of women warriors was probably a fantasy, inspired by ancient Greek legends of the Amazons. The European explorers believed these women lived in the jungle to the south, which is why they named the great river in Brazil the Amazon and the southernmost territory of Venezuela is called Amazonas.

But it was the myth of El Dorado that impelled adventurers from Spain, Holland, Germany, England, and other countries to risk—and often lose—their lives in pursuit of fabulous wealth.

Early Towns   Between 1545 and 1589, the Spaniards founded numerous towns throughout the northern valleys and coastlands.

Founding a town in those days meant setting up whatever defenses seemed necessary—if the Indians were hostile, this might be a wall of stout wooden poles stuck upright in the ground—and drawing with the point of the sword in the dirt the location of streets and the main buildings. Sometimes a plan would be drawn on paper, and a few of these early plans still survive.

The towns were set up like the military camps the Romans had built when they conquered Spain many centuries earlier. In the center there would be a rectangular open space, called the *plaza*, for parades and military exercises. The commander's residence faced this *plaza*, around which the founders of the town laid out a grid of straight streets.

Later the Spanish issued a set of laws known as the Ordinances of the Indies, stipulating that all new towns should be set up this way, and even prescribing the proper dimensions for the Plaza de Armas (Square of Weapons, or Military Square). According to the ordinances, a church had to be built on the opposite side of the *plaza* from the commander's, or governor's house. The crown considered Christianizing the Indians as important as intimidating them with weapons. As the town developed, the *plaza* would be used not only for military ceremonies, but also for church festivals and, the rest of the time, as an open marketplace. The towns founded in this period included Tocuyo (1545), Barquisimeto (1552), Valencia (1555), Mérida (1558), and Trujillo (also 1558).

These little towns were constantly threatened by raids from Indians, who were angered because the Spaniards had been enslaving their brothers and sisters to sell to colonies in the Caribbean and had forced others to work in mines and agriculture. Guaicaipuro, chief of the Teques, and his allies in the north central valleys attacked the Spanish gold mines and settlements. Meanwhile, in 1561, a renegade Spanish conquistador from Peru, Lope de Aguirre, landed on Margarita Island. Apparently driven mad by the hardships in the jungle and his futile search for El Dorado, Aguirre led his little band of soldiers in a rampage of slaughter and destruction from Margarita to Barquisimeto, where Spanish troops finally caught up to him and killed him.

After Aguirre's death, Santiago de León de Caracas was founded in 1567. *Caracas* was an Indian word for a plant, similar to yucca, that was common in the area, but the Spaniards thought it was the name of the tribe and the place. Maracaibo—another Indian word—was also founded in 1567, and Caracas's port town of La Guaira in 1589.

It would take almost two hundred years, but Caracas was destined to become the economic and political center of the colony, for several reasons. Although the mountain barrier made it difficult to reach the sea, it also helped keep the pirates away. (Not completely, however: The English pirate Amayas Preston found an unguarded pass in 1595 and sacked the town.) Also, because of the 3,000-foot (900-meter) elevation, the temperature was more pleasant than in the hot coastal towns. The valley had numerous rivers and streams, and there was even a small amount of gold to be mined. But what would turn out to be most important was that the green, well-watered hills were ideal for growing cacao.

Dancers in Cumaná in the early 1800's, from an 1842 travel book published in Barcelona, Spain.

The Mature Colony

The Agricultural Economy

Once they had given up their dreams of El Dorado, the colonists settled down to make a living from the fertile soil. Most of what they grew or raised was consumed within the colony, but there were also exports for trade—mostly with Spain and the other Spanish colonies, including New Granada (now Colombia), Mexico, and the Caribbean. In the middle 1600's, Venezuela's main exports were cacao, wheat, tobacco, and animal hides, and the colony also exported cotton, indigo, gold, and copper. Of all these, the biggest money-maker by far was cacao.

Economic Regions

The wealthiest region of the colony was the area around Caracas and the fertile valleys of Aragua, where almost anything that grows in Venezuela could be grown. This region's trade, through the port of La Guaira, was mainly with Mexico—which bought a lot of the cacao—and Europe.

The Chocolate Tree

Chocolate is made by roasting and grinding the seeds from the large, yellowish-orange pods of the cacao tree. The tree is native to the Americas, and chocolate was completely unknown in Europe before the seventeenth century. "Cocoa," as the English called it, was introduced to Europe by the Spaniards, and by the late 1600's was being sold for high prices in specialty shops. Some of these, such as London's Cocoa Tree Club on St. James's Street, became famous political discussion clubs.

The tree grows on shady hillsides in the tropics, the main producing areas in Venezuela being in the Aragua valleys in the center of the country and the eastern hills around Cumaná. In colonial days, it was grown and harvested by black slaves. The Venezuelan planters sold their cacao mainly to Spain, which then supplied the European luxury market, and to Spanish colonists in Mexico. Dutch smugglers also bought Venezuelan cacao illegally from their colonies in Curaçao and Aruba, and this became the basis of the famous Dutch chocolate industry. Although cacao was grown in other parts of the New World as well, the Venezuelan variety was especially prized because it was not as bitter and so required less sugar. The Caracas plantation owners became the richest people in the colony, accustomed to going about in fine carriages and wearing expensive clothing. The poorer people gave them the nickname *mantuanos*, not because they were from Mantua but because the women wore very elaborate *mantas*, fine Spanish woven shawls, which nobody else could afford.

But there were two other major economic regions, operating independently of Caracas. In the west, Coro and Maracaibo had their own trade routes, between Mexico and the Caribbean and the western Llanos and the Andes, as far away as Bogotá. Their customers included not only authorized dealers, but also Dutch and English smugglers. They also exported cacao, along with tobacco and other products.

In the east, exports from the ports of Cumaná and Barcelona included hides and cattle from the eastern Llanos, to their south, and more cacao. All these regions also produced many other foods, such as bananas, corn, and the many root vegetables (yucca, ñame, malanga, and so on) that are an important part of the local diet, but these were consumed locally or sometimes traded from one region of Venezuela to another.

In the interior, on the banks of the Orinoco, Franciscan, Capuchin,

This wheat-flour mill in San Lázaro, Trujillo State, is an example of colonial technology: The control wheel at the right opens and closes a channel of water (beneath the floor) that drives the grinding stone. Vladimir Sersa

and other missionaries, mostly from Spain, had established missions that Christianized and Hispanicized the Indians—that is, taught them Spanish language and customs, such as wearing clothes. Some of these became prosperous agricultural and cattle-raising communities. But they had even less contact with Coro, Caracas, and Cumaná than those three had with each other.

The Bourbon Reforms

In two centuries of operation, the Spanish colonial system became very unwieldy and inefficient, with much duplication of functions (two or more officials assigned to do the same thing), too many layers of bureaucracy for approval of any new project, and a lack of responsiveness to changes within the colonies. By the 1700's, the task was no longer to subdue the Indians but to develop the economies so that they could bring in more revenues to Spain. But too many of the colonial businesspeople were avoiding the Spanish authorities altogether and dealing with smugglers. Military defenses were obsolete, too, and there was increasing danger from raiders from other nations.

Now, under the Bourbons, the family that had come to power in Spain, the monarchy carried out a number of reforms to update and streamline its colonial system. In 1728, as part of this program, the Spanish crown granted important government powers and a monopoly on trading Venezuelan cacao to the Compañía Guipuzcoana, a Basque trading enterprise. It also became known as the Caracas Company, because it centered its whole administration in that city. During the period of its rule, other government institutions were developed in Caracas, such as the *cabildo* (town council) of local farmers and busi-nessmen, and a royal *audiencia* (court), with jurisdiction over the whole country. In 1777, the crown created the Captaincy General of Venezu-ela, based in Caracas, with political and military authority over the whole country.

The Customs House of the Compañía Guipuzcoana, or Caracas Company, still stands in the port of La Guaira. Vladimir Sersa

In some ways the Caracas Company's monopoly worked better than the similar arrangement two hundred years before with the Welsers; it managed to bring the three main economic regions together under one administration, creating the framework for modern Venezuela. But its pricing policies, administrative inefficiencies, and harsh and arbitrary actions increased the tensions between the colonists and their Spanish rulers.

The Company by law was to be the exclusive purchaser of Venezuelan cacao, which it could then sell at international market rates. It was supposed to use the profits to improve defense and public administration in Venezuela. Naturally, the Company set the price for their purchases of cacao very low. The *mantuanos* were outraged.

There had been several minor slave revolts, and the growing population of free (nonslave) blacks and browns had many grievances against the system. However, the first important protest by the white Creoles came in 1749. A small-town colonial official named Juan Francisco de León got fed up when the Company gave his job to a Basque, and he gathered a group to march to Caracas to protest the Company's privileges. The protest grew into an armed confrontation in which León and his men were overwhelmed by Spanish troops. Several were killed, and León was sent off to prison in Spain. This was the first major sign of a split between the white colonials and the Spanish authorities.

Signs of Trouble

In 1795, José Leonardo Chirino, a free black sharecropper, led a rising of blacks in the province of Coro, calling for an end to slavery and to certain taxes. Punishment of these rebels was far more severe than against León: Some were decapitated, and the leader was taken to Caracas to be hanged and quartered (pulled apart by four horses).

Sales of slaves continued in the early Republic; this scene is from a travel book published in Spain in 1842.

In 1797, two whites from La Guaira, Manuel Gual and José María España, conspired to set up an independent republic of Venezuela. Several dark-skinned Venezuelans were also involved. But the plot was discovered, and the leaders fled to avoid arrest.

In 1806, Francisco de Miranda, a fifty-six-year-old soldier, diplomat, and world traveler who had been out of his native Venezuela for many years, organized an expeditionary force in New York, with American, English, French, and Irish volunteers, to invade Venezuela. He expected the Venezuelans to welcome him and rise against Spain in imitation of the American, French, and Haitian revolutionaries, but instead they ran away and called the soldiers. After a defeat at Puerto Cabello and a very hostile response from the locals at Coro, he called the whole thing off and took refuge in the Antilles.

Venezuela might have had to wait a long time for its independence if it had not been for events far across the sea. In 1808, Napoleon invaded Spain and imprisoned the king, Fernando VII. Napoleon then named his own brother, Joseph Bonaparte, as the new king. The Royalists, those loyal to Fernando, fought back against the invaders in *guerrillas* (Spanish for "little wars"), coordinated by a *junta* (supreme central council). King Joseph then sent new governors to the colonies to oust those of the previous regime. The colonials were undecided as to whom to obey, and groups pushing to revolt against the new authorities began to meet and conspire in Caracas and other colonial capitals.

To that point, with all its problems, the colony had been working fairly well for people who owned property, and the others were not yet organized enough or angry enough to revolt. But then in 1810 it looked as though the last stronghold of the Spanish resistance, in Cádiz, was about to fall to the French. If the colonials did not act quickly, they were likely to become permanent French colonies. There were a lot of problems with this idea, not the least of which was that it would bring them into war with England—the colony's best trading partner, but the enemy of Napoleon. The crisis was felt throughout the Spanish empire, from Mexico to Buenos Aires, but it was the *mantuanos* of Caracas who were the first to act.

The First Republic

On April 19, 1810, the white elite of Caracas convened a *cabildo abierto*—an open city council meeting. They deposed King Joseph's representative and set up a *junta* to govern Venezuela in the name of Fernando VII. Since Fernando was in prison, this amounted to declaring independence.

The members of the new *junta* made speeches, abolished the slave trade (but without freeing existing slaves), and settled down to their main concern, cutting taxes. These cautious businessmen had no idea that they had started the country on a process that would take it through thirteen years of war, in which almost all their property would be destroyed and they and their families would be killed, exiled or—the most astounding of all—turned into heroes.

On July 5, 1811, they took the next step and declared Venezuela's independence from Spain—but without the signatures of representatives from Coro, Maracaibo, and Guayana. The *junta* then drafted a constitution, modeled on that of the United States, which was approved on December 21, 1811, creating the first Republic, which some Venezuelan historians have called the "Patria Boba" (Dumb Country), because it made so many stupid mistakes.

To their surprise, few outside of Caracas recognized their authority, and even there it was shaky.

At this moment, the independence movement was a project of the white elite of one city, Caracas. It was the biggest city in the country with, at most, 42,000 inhabitants in 1810—about the size of Spartanburg, South Carolina, today.

In 1810, there were probably between 900,000 and one million people living in Venezuela, according to different estimates. About half, some 496,000, were in the province of Caracas—a very large area, including most of the modern states of Miranda, Aragua, Guárico, Yaracuy, Cojedes, Lara, and Falcón.

In the whole of Venezuela, native-born whites made up about 19 percent of the population, and Spanish-born another 1 percent. Thus only 20 percent of the population was white.

The most numerous racial group were *pardos* (browns), "free" (that is, not slave) people of mixed African and European or African and Indian ancestry. They were 45 percent of the population. These included sharecroppers, businesspeople, craftsmen, and laborers. Some of them were prosperous, and all had business dealings with the white elite. While many *pardos* had been unhappy with Spanish colonial rule, it wasn't clear to all of them that they would be better off under the Creoles.

Free blacks were another 4 percent of the population.

Black slaves were about 10 percent of the total population, concentrated mostly in the north central part of the country. They were mostly agricultural workers, and others were domestic servants.

Runaway slaves, or *cimarrones*, were about 3 percent of the population. Some of these had set up communities in the northern hills or, in many cases, in the Llanos to the south, where they lived as cattle hunters.

The remaining 18 percent were Indians, about half of them working almost as slaves in missions, others living free on the Llanos like the *cimarrones*, and the rest—deep in the forests—having almost no contact with whites or blacks.

The white Creoles in Caracas stood the most to gain from ending colonial taxes and trade restrictions. But, given the demography, independence would not work if the *negros* (blacks) and *pardos* actively opposed it. This was one reason the new *junta* abolished the slave trade. They did not abolish slavery, since the wealth of the *mantuanos* depended on it and also because they were afraid of provoking a black uprising such as had occurred in Haiti just six years earlier.

The republic collapsed very quickly. Coro, the Guayana, and other regions refused to accept Caracas's leadership. Francisco de Miranda, who had returned to Venezuela to take command, found himself in a civil war as he put down revolts. He gave the young *mantuano* Simón Bolívar, then only twenty-eight years old, his first military command, the fortress at Puerto Cabello, but Bolívar lost it when Spanish prisoners in the fortress revolted and took it over for Spain. Then an earthquake struck (March 12, 1812), destroying large parts of Caracas and other cities that had declared independence and killing some twelve thousand people—the Royalists interpreted this as a punishment by God.

The people of Coro welcomed and even joined the small contingent of 230 Spanish troops, under the command of Domingo Monteverde, that landed to put down the rebellion. Marching east to Caracas, Monteverde's scorched-earth strategy and his call on the slaves to rise against their Creole masters made Miranda decide not to continue the fight. In July 1812, he crossed the mountain to La Guaira to take a ship into exile. Bolívar and another officer caught up with him there and, blaming their former commander for the debacle, arrested him at gunpoint and turned him over to the Spanish general. Miranda was imprisoned, but Bolívar was permitted to go into exile. Miranda, today considered a national hero and forerunner of Venezuelan independence, died a prisoner in Spain.

But the war wasn't over. The Royalists were going to have as hard a time holding this country together as had the republic. In the east, a patriot army under Santiago Mariño held and even gained territory, and another patriot force under Juan Bautista Arismendi held out on Margarita. And the crisis had also unleashed another social force, the new-found strength of the country's nonwhite people, which would affect the country's history in violent and contradictory ways.

The Struggle for Independence: 1813–1830

"The Amazing Campaign" and the Second Republic

The neighboring colony of New Granada (modern-day Colombia) had also declared independence, and Bolívar went there to offer his services. With a tiny army of seventy men, and very little support from the rebel government in New Granada, he set out to recapture Caracas in what has come to be called "La Campaña Admirable" (The Amazing Campaign).

What made it amazing was that he and his men got so far so quickly. They crossed the border at Cúcuta in April 1813, and defeated the first Royalist contingent they found. By now the colonials were more frightened by the Spanish general, Monteverde, than by the idea of independence, and men flocked to join the young captain, so the army kept

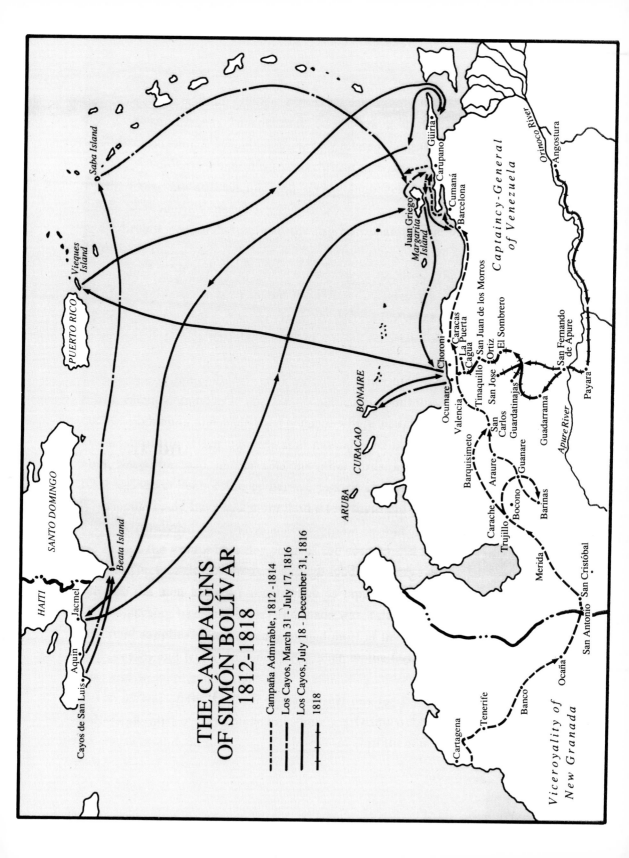

THE CAMPAIGNS OF SIMÓN BOLÍVAR 1812-1818

Campaña Admirable, 1812-1814

Los Cayos, March 31 - July 17, 1816

Los Cayos, July 18 - December 31, 1816

1818

HAITI

SANTO DOMINGO

PUERTO RICO

Cayos de San Luis

Aquin

Jacmel

Beata Island

Vieques Island

Saba Island

ARUBA

CURACAO

BONAIRE

Captaincy-General of Venezuela

Orinoco River

Angostura

Güiria

Carúpano

Cumaná

Barcelona

Juan Griego

Margarita Island

Ocumare

Choroni

Caracas

La Puerta

Cagua

Valencia

Tinaquillo

San Juan de los Morros

El Sombrero

Ortiz

San José

Guardatinajas

San Carlos

Guadarrama

Apure River

San Fernando de Apure

Payara

Barquisimeto

Araure

Guanare

San

Bocono

Barinas

Carache

Trujillo

Merida

San Cristóbal

San Antonio

Ocaña

Banco

Tenerife

Cartagena

Viceroyality of New Granada

Simón Bolívar, from an engraving in the collection of the John Boulton Foundation (Caracas).

growing as it galloped from town to town. The reason for the rush was that Monteverde had destroyed almost everything, so that Bolívar's only hope of paying his troops or even of feeding them very well was to get to Caracas. When he reached Mérida, the town council proclaimed him "Liberator," the title he would use for the rest of his career.

In June, in the midst of this campaign, he issued his famous decree of "War to the Death": Any Spaniard caught would be put to death, even if he were neutral, unless he actively aided the revolt, but the lives of Venezuelans would be respected even if they did nothing. This cruel decree resulted in the execution of scores of Spanish-born civilians who wanted nothing to do with the war, and the seizure of their property to finance the revolt. It was mainly a response to the Royalist killings of innocent Venezuelans and the seizure of their property. The net result was a great deal of bloodshed and property destruction on both sides.

Bolívar and his now-enlarged army seized Caracas on August 6. Santiago Mariño, who had been planning to do the same thing from his base in Oriente, accepted Bolívar's authority. Bolívar assumed command of the government, and in October the city council of Caracas named him Captain General of the troops of the Second Republic and confirmed his title of Liberator.

It would not last. Now another commander, José Tomás Boves, declared his own "War to the Death," this time against the proindependence forces.

"The Terrible Year"

The year 1814 is known in Venezuelan history as "The Terrible Year," mostly because of Boves. Born in 1783, the same year as Bolívar, José Tomás Boves had come to Venezuela from Asturias, Spain, as a sailor and had settled in the Llanos, where he became a ranch foreman. When war broke out during the short-lived first republic, he sought a command with the rebels but was rebuffed—possibly because he was too poorly educated and rough mannered for them. Now, whether out of resentment, opportunism, or just the love of a fight, he declared his loyalty to Spain and created an army of *llaneros* to make war on the Creoles.

Although Boves himself was fair-skinned and fair-haired, he exploited the *llaneros'* racial resentments to stir them up against the republic, crying "Death to the whites!" in furious cavalry charges. At ranches and farms, he would encourage his men to loot anything they fancied and to kill the men and rape the women. Black slaves from these places then joined his army, either because they wanted to or because they were afraid not to—Boves and his men were very frightening. By calling on the slaves to rise up and fight against the republic, not only

The Llaneros *as Revolutionary Force*

The Llanos had been on the edge of the colony, populated by only a few towns and having no influence on political or economic decisions. Cattle, horses, and donkeys, first brought over by the Spaniards, had gone wild and multiplied there, and some of the country's wildest people lived there also.

The first *llaneros* were Indians of the plains, who learned to catch and ride the wild horses and lived mainly by hunting cattle, which they would kill with lances made of a long, sturdy pole and a sharpened bone tied to the end. Some of them worked as cattle herders for whites, who used black slaves as foremen. Runaway slaves, or *cimarrones*, had also established themselves in the Llanos, learning from the Indians how to survive, as did some whites and mixed-race people. The Llanos were the place to go for anybody who wanted to get away from civilized life, to escape the racial discrimination of the white-run cities, or to evade the law. Indians, blacks, Spaniards, and mixtures of all three would spend practically their whole lives on horseback, living on wild cattle they hunted down with lances or wrestled to the ground by grabbing their tails—a favorite sport of the *llaneros*.

As long as the colonial system remained stable, the *llaneros* stayed out of its way. Some of them worked on ranches; to handle

was Boves increasing the size of his army, he was destroying the patriots' capacity to produce food. This would be a critical problem throughout the wars.

At this time, there were very few Spanish troops involved—the armies on both sides were made up almost entirely of Venezuelans.

An 1827 English print shows "Lancers of the Plains of Apure, Attacking Spanish Troops."

these men, the foreman had to be at least as skillful a horseman and bull wrestler as they. But the revolutionary events in the towns on the coast upset their way of life.

During the war years, people of all backgrounds and races took refuge in the Llanos, some of them adapting quickly to the hard life and all of them ready to do desperate things to survive. Fighting forces from the Llanos would be decisive in finally winning liberation for Venezuela, and would continue to dominate its politics for most of the century.

There were blacks, whites, Indians, and mixed people on both sides of the war, and in one famous battle, the fighting suddenly stopped because the black patriots and black Royalists refused to kill each other. However, because Boves promised freedom to black slaves and the patriots did not, there were more of them in his *llanero* cavalry.

On June 14, Bolívar and Mariño joined their best troops to stop Boves at a mountain pass called La Puerta, near Villa de Cura, only about 90 miles (150 kilometers) from Caracas. The patriots were routed, and the commanders and the remnants of their troops rushed back to Caracas. Bolívar ordered the evacuation of the capital, commandeering every available oxcart and wagon to carry families and everything of value for a trek east to Barcelona, which was still in patriot hands. Boves took Valencia on July 10, and on July 16 he entered Caracas, before setting out to wipe out what remained of the patriots in the east. Bolívar and Mariño made a deal with a pirate captain, Bianchi, loaded all the wealth they'd brought from Caracas on one of his ships, and fled the country. All the other refugees who could also escaped, some of them to Trinidad. General Manuel Piar, who had been fighting in the area, declared Bolívar and Mariño to be deserters and tried to capture them to have them shot—but he got there too late.

Boves, meanwhile, kept coming. He may have been deranged, like the mad Aguirre 250 years earlier. He was certainly as cruel. When he captured Barcelona, now crammed with refugees, he ordered a ball. Musicians were rounded up and forced to play, and women were forced to dance with his rough soldiers while, outside by the riverbank, their husbands were executed one by one.

Boves died as he had lived. At the little town of Urica, in the hills southeast of Barcelona, he ran up against a lance. His troops won the battle, but they would never again have such a commander.

Return of Spanish Troops

Meanwhile, there had been big changes in Spain. Napoleon's armies had finally been driven out by the Spanish resistance, with help from the Duke of Wellington's English troops, and Fernando VII was back on the the throne. A stupid and stubborn man, Fernando rescinded all the reforms he'd agreed to in order to get the Spaniards to accept his return, and then he thought it would be a simple matter to put down the revolt in the colonies by sending veteran Spanish troops.

In 1815, Pablo Morillo, a general who had fought against Napoleon, arrived in Venezuela with over 10,000 troops—a very large force, considering that in Venezuela, four or five hundred men could be called an army, and that by this time the patriot forces were reduced to scattered groups of ten or twenty.

Bolívar, in Jamaica, was discouraged and wrote that he thought that Morillo would soon have the entire colony back under Royalist control if he didn't make any major mistakes. But Morillo had already made one. He had no use for the rough, unruly men who had fought with Boves, and sent them packing. They drifted back into the Llanos in small bands, scavenging as they could.

Morillo then found himself facing a problem he recognized. When he and his compatriots had fought against Napoleon's army of occupation, they had fought in small bands to harass and attack the French at every opportunity. Now the Venezuelans were using *guerrilla* tactics against him, in the Llanos.

Some of these were *llaneros* who had fought with Boves, and had now turned against the Royalist troops with their white-and-blue uniforms, muskets, and bayonets. The *llaneros* had no uniforms at all; in fact many of them rode stark naked, and their weapons at first were nothing more than the primitive *llanero* cattle prod, turned into a lance by tying a sharp point to the end. But they knew the terrain, and they were tough and dangerous. They also stood up against the tropical diseases much better than Morillo's men.

In the western Llanos of Apure, the *llanero* bands were gathering around a muscular, illiterate, 25-year-old ranch foreman named José Antonio Páez. In the east, Manuel Piar had put together an army and was fighting his way to the Orinoco River.

Success at Last: The Base in the Guayana

Piar, born in 1782, was a capable, intelligent, and ambitious commander who had served under Mariño but now had struck out on his own. He created an army out of all the diverse people he found in the Llanos, including Indians, who fought as a separate corps using bows and arrows, and drove the Spaniards from wide areas along the banks of the Orinoco.

Piar was a mulatto, one of many among the leaders of the liberation armies. Such men had found their opportunities for wealth and political influence very limited in the old colonial society. The black, mulatto, and Indian soldiers in the liberation armies had a different stake in the war than the whites. For them, it was not enough to replace Spanish rulers with *mantuanos*. They demanded a more open society, and symbolic of that openness would be the abolition of slavery.

Bolívar had called for the abolition of slavery several times, but other white leaders whose support he needed had opposed abolition. However, any slave who joined the army was guaranteed his freedom.

How Piar's color influenced his attitudes on slavery and other issues we can only guess, because he did not leave an extensive written record. But his color did seem to make him especially popular with the non-white troops, who were the majority. For this reason, he was a potential threat to the whites who hoped to continue running an independent Venezuela.

Bolívar, in exile in Jamaica, wrote an open "Letter to a Gentleman of Jamaica," in which he analyzed the ethnic politics of Spanish America. The Indians and blacks, he wrote, were by nature peaceful, gentle people. Boves and the other Spanish generals had urged them to pillage, murder, and steal, and "dazzled them with superstitious doctrines in favor of the Spanish side," but even so had had to threaten them to get them to make war.

"No, sir," Bolívar wrote, "domestic strife in America has never come from racial differences; it has risen from divergences of political opinion and from the personal ambition of a few men, just as it has in other countries."

In general this may have been true, but some of the "divergences of political opinion" surely had to do with the divergences of opportunity for people of different colors.

Bolívar next went to Haiti, then the only black republic in the world, where slaves had liberated themselves by defeating armies sent by Napoleon himself. The president, Alexandre Pétion, not only welcomed the refugee liberator but gave him the weapons and ships he needed to organize a new expedition to Venezuela. Pétion insisted that, when Bolívar won, one of the first things he must do was to free the slaves of his country, and Bolívar readily agreed.

After a debacle in his attempted invasion at Ocumare on the coast of Venezuela, Bolívar returned to Haiti, where Pétion outfitted him again. This time he went to Barcelona, now in the hands of the patriots, and from there rode to join Piar in the Guayana. Despite their past difficulties, relations between the two men seemed to be very cordial. Bolívar took over command of the army that Piar had assembled, with Piar as his second in command, and together they finally drove the Spaniards out of Angostura. Key to this victory was the patriot navy, commanded by Luis Brion, also a mulatto, a merchant from Curaçao who used his personal wealth to put together a fleet that helped keep Royalist reinforcements from coming up the Orinoco. The Army of Liberation now had control of the Guayana.

But then, when Piar tried to leave, he was caught, accused of "desertion" (the same charge he had leveled at Bolívar two years earlier),

Foreign Legionaries

The end of the Napoleonic wars in Europe had another effect on the fighting in Venezuela besides the arrival of Morillo. Thousands of soldiers were now unemployed, and some had already found their way to South America. Bolívar sent agents to England and Ireland to recruit a "British Legion" and "Irish Legion." Baron Johannes von Uslar-Gleichen of Hanover, Germany, raised a legion of three hundred German veterans, who were incorporated into the British Legion. The Uslars are even today a prominent family in Venezuela. There were also French, Belgians, and other Europeans.

The legionaries came expecting glory and regular pay, and quite a number still had romantic ideas of finding El Dorado. But they also believed that the struggle in Venezuela would advance the cause of liberty everywhere.

When the legionaries saw Bolívar and his half-naked lancers, some of them began to think the whole liberation idea was absurd. But it wasn't. With little more than these rough plainsmen, the food

court-martialed, and shot. All this was done by officers loyal to Bolívar, who did not himself visibly intervene. The Liberator watched the firing squad from a balcony in the *plaza* of Angostura, and according to witnesses was very saddened. There is a plaque on the wall where Piar was shot, quoting Bolívar's high praise of his general and giving the date and hour of the execution: October 16, 1817, at five in the afternoon. Where had Piar been going? Why didn't Bolívar save him? It may have been that Bolívar feared he would try to raise the black and brown

resources of the Guayana, and his own strong will and intelligence, Bolívar would in the next seven years bring about the collapse of Spanish power in America. Armies under his command would expel the Royalists from what are today six countries: Venezuela, Colombia, Panama, Ecuador, Peru, and Bolivia. Many of these legionaries, even some who had originally just come for the money and the adventure, stayed and fought heroically in these campaigns.

Two of the best-known foreigners with the patriots had come not with the Legions, but on their own. The Scot General Gregor MacGregor, very brave and usually very drunk, fought in the east with Piar, and General Daniel Florencio O'Leary, a young Irishman (born in 1800) who seems to have been very sober, became Bolívar's aide-de-camp and one of his earliest biographers. In the later years of the struggle, there were even Spanish officers with the patriot forces, men who had volunteered because they opposed kingships and empires and wanted to take part in the creation of a new kind of government, whose authority would come from the people. A new kind of government did emerge, but not what they had imagined.

(negro and pardo) troops against him, but if there was strong evidence against Piar, it has been lost.

Final Liberation

The patriots convened a Congress in Angostura. Bolívar inaugurated it with a powerful speech, interpreting the chaotic events of the past few years, outlining his theory of government, and declaring his vision for the future. In essence, he called for a republic with indirect elections and a powerful chief executive, to keep the fickle passions of the masses in check. He also spoke of his plans to unite Venezuela and New Granada, both of which were still occupied by Royalist troops.

First, though, he had to deal with the continuing war in Venezuela. There had been times when Mariño's men in Barcelona, blockaded by the Royalists, had had nothing to eat but bananas and chocolate—pretty good once in a while, but not as a steady diet. At other times, in the Llanos, the men had tried to eat their saddles (which were nothing more than pieces of rawhide). Now that they had the cattle lands of the southern Llanos and the Guayana under their control, for the first time since they were driven out by Boves in 1813, the patriots would have enough to eat—even if it was just meat without salt.

Páez was the patriots' greatest master of warfare in the Llanos, and Bolívar came to depend on him more and more. In April, Páez inflicted heavy losses on Morillo's men in a battle at Queseras del Medio. But Bolívar had bigger ambitions. He decided it was time to cross the Andes, into New Granada.

Starting out with some thirteen hundred infantrymen, eight hundred cavalry and their horses, and—although these weren't counted on the official roster—the soldiers' female companions, this army set out for the most difficult pass through the Andes, where the Spaniards would be least expecting them. They had been eating nothing but tough beef, but now they were cheered up by the arrival of a shipment of bananas and salt. When they got to the mountains, the *llaneros* were amazed. As O'Leary described it, "Men used in their Plains to cross torrential rivers, to tame wild horses and to win in straight fights over bulls, tigers and crocodiles, felt chastened by such strange nature. . . . Many deserted."

Nobody was dressed adequately for the cold of the heights. As they climbed peak after peak, the thin air gave many of them *soroche*, a mountain sickness that made them nauseous and weak. They blamed their diarrhea on the cold rain that was falling constantly. Horses and mules fell and blocked the path of the troops coming up behind. But the *llaneros* and British legionaries struggled on. At one point O'Leary, slumped to the ground exhausted, noticed a little group huddled together and asked what was happening. "Oh, nothing," said one of the men from the Rifles Battalion; "just one of the women giving birth." The next morning, there she was at the tag end, carrying her baby.

Bolívar, tireless, kept urging everyone on, helping to pull the baggage or push a dead horse out of the way. Somehow, soaked, starving, exhausted, the army—or most of it, without their horses—finally got across. Among those who didn't make it were a fourth of the Englishmen. The people in New Granada gave them a warm welcome, food, and fresh *alpargatas* (sandals), and Granadine men rushed to join them. With this army, Bolívar defeated the Royalists at Boyacá, which broke Royalist power in the colony. New Granada was now liberated.

When Bolívar returned to Angostura later that year, he got the Congress to proclaim the larger republic that until now had only been his dream. It included what were then the provinces of Venezuela, New Granada, and Quito (later renamed Ecuador). He called the new country Colombia, in honor of Christopher Columbus. Congress elected Bolívar to be its president.

In the next two years, Bolívar would succeed in uniting the three provinces. But the union would be shaky, and despite everything Bolívar could do, they eventually split up into separate countries. New Granada kept for itself the name "Colombia." For this reason historians now call Bolívar's creation Gran Colombia (Greater Colombia).

The war in Venezuela continued, but now the Spaniards were on the defensive. In June 1821, Bolívar, supported by Mariño and Páez, de-

The Quinta Anauco in San Bernardino, now the Museum of Colonial Art, was the country home of the Marqués del Toro, a Venezuelan-born planter who used a Spanish title of nobility but supported Bolívar and independence.   Vladimir Sersa

feated the Royalist army at Carabobo, near Valencia, in the last major battle for Venezuela. In the next year, the Royalist troops would be driven out of the whole country except Puerto Cabello, which would finally fall to Páez in 1823. All in all, the liberation of Venezuela took thirteen years of almost continual warfare. Its industries and agriculture were destroyed, most of its people were destitute, and there had been almost no schooling during all that time. Furthermore, everywhere in the country there were armed veterans with no other skill but warfare.

Completing the Job: Venezuelans Abroad

From the crossing of the Andes in 1819 until his death eleven years later, Bolívar's theater of operations would be not just Venezuela but all of northern South America. And everywhere the Liberator went, he took Venezuelan officers and troops, until there were Venezuelan detachments from Panama to Cochabamba, Bolivia.

After winning control of Ecuador in 1822, Bolívar met General José de San Martín, who had freed Chile and the Peruvian coast and named himself Protector of Peru. San Martín decided to leave the remainder of the fighting to Bolívar, and sailed to France. Bolívar then became Dictator—meaning supreme commander, a word he preferred to Protector. The victory of Ayacucho, won by the young Venezuelan General Sucre in 1824, completed the liberation of Peru and of the province of Upper Peru. This battle marked the end of Spanish power everywhere in America, except for the islands of Cuba and Puerto Rico. Upper Peru was renamed "Bolivia" in Bolívar's honor in 1825, and Sucre became its first president—although continuing to recognize Bolívar as the supreme chief. (See *The Land and People of Bolivia.*)

As president of (Gran) Colombia and Dictator of Peru, Bolívar's nominal authority now extended over a vast area, covering what are today six countries and part of a seventh. These were Venezuela, New Granada (now Colombia), Panama (a part of New Granada), Ecuador, Peru, Bolivia, and much of northern Chile (territory that then belonged to Bolivia and Peru). Venezuelan troops and officers occupied key positions in all these lands, along with armies drawn from the local populations. Sucre, president of Bolivia, for example, was from Cumaná.

In his imagination, Bolívar went even further; he dreamed of uniting

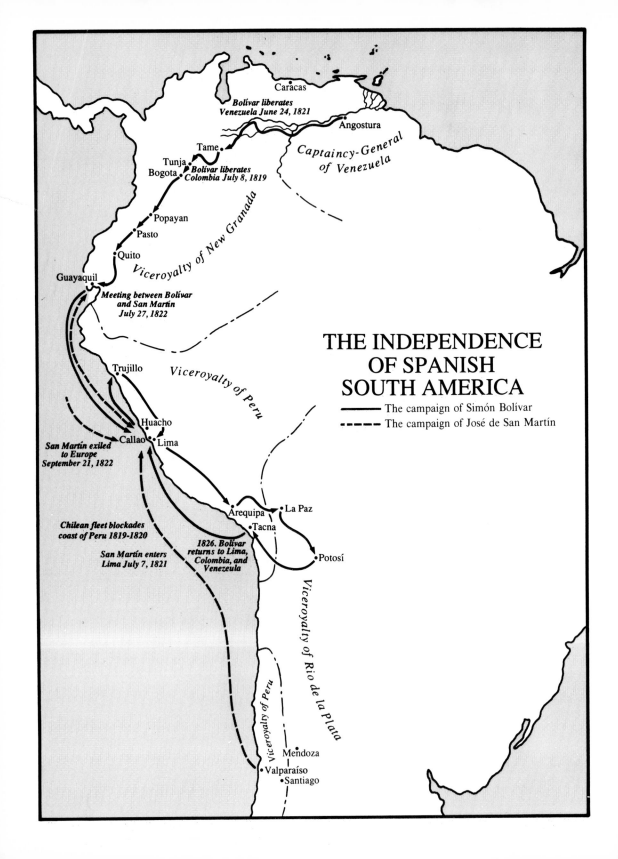

Caracas

Bolívar liberates
Venezuela June 24, 1821

Angostura

Tame

Captaincy-General
of Venezuela

Tunja
Bogota
Bolívar liberates
Colombia July 8, 1819

Popayan

Pasto

Quito

Viceroyalty of New Granada

Guayaquil

Meeting between Bolívar
and San Martín
July 27, 1822

Trujillo

Viceroyalty of Peru

Huacho

Callao Lima

San Martín exiled
to Europe
September 21, 1822

Chilean fleet blockades
coast of Peru 1819-1820

San Martín enters
Lima July 7, 1821

1826. Bolívar
returns to Lima,
Colombia, and
Venezeula

Arequipa • La Paz

Tacna

• Potosí

THE INDEPENDENCE
OF SPANISH
SOUTH AMERICA

——— The campaign of Simón Bolívar

- - - - The campaign of José de San Martín

Viceroyalty of Rio de la Plata

Viceroyalty of Peru

Mendoza

Valparaíso
Santiago

all of Spanish America, from Mexico to Argentina, in a grand federation with its capital in Panama.

But as Bolívar's political and military authority expanded over an ever-widening territory, it became more and more difficult to exercise real control anywhere. In Venezuela, Páez had made himself the civil and political chief of the country in 1826, defying orders from the central government in Bogotá that he give up command and report to the capital. Bolívar had to rush from Peru to Bogotá, and from there to Caracas, where he personally took over the government of Venezuela for six months—from January to June of 1827—before returning to Bogotá. There he found so much disorder that he had himself named Dictator of Colombia, with greater powers than he had had as president. He thought he had patched things up with Páez, but in 1829 Páez supported another separatist rebellion and led Venezuela out of Colombia. Bolívar's dream of a united South America was falling apart.

All this rushing from one city to another, on horseback through mountains, jungles, deserts, and plains, over distances that even today take hours to fly, had taken a toll on Bolívar's small, tough body. His health began to fail, his hair was turning white, and he was rapidly losing weight. There were attempts to assassinate him—not by Royalists, who were now out of the picture, but by people who had been his allies but now wanted him out of the way. In 1830, he resigned his dictatorship and presidency and announced that he was going into exile.

He was probably expecting the politicians in Bogotá to plead with him to stay on, as they had done before, but this time there was only silence, and he began his last sad journey to the coast. On the way he learned that Sucre, who he had hoped would be his political heir, had been murdered—a terrible emotional blow to him. He reached the house of a supporter near Santa Marta, on the Caribbean coast, weakened, shriveled, and embittered, with only a few faithful officers and servants, but

Bolívar, Man and Image

Today Simón Bolívar is honored everywhere in Venezuela. Every city has a Plaza Bolívar with his statue, and his portrait is on Venezuela's currency—which is called the *bolívar*. The largest state bears his name, the largest city in that state is Ciudad Bolívar, and the biggest iron lode is Cerro Bolívar. In speeches and newspaper columns, he is not only "Father of the Country" and "Liberator," he is called the country's "Guiding Spirit." He is more than a hero. In many households he is treated as a saint, or perhaps even a god.

In the shacks of poor blacks in Barlovento in the 1960's and 1970's, a researcher noted that "the walls almost always have a few lithographs of saints, calendars, a portrait of Simón Bolívar, some family photos or a little altar adorned with candles, artificial flowers and holy water."

All of this is quite remarkable, considering that Bolívar was called a tyrant by political leaders in Venezuela in the last years of his life and that they rejoiced at news of his death in 1830.

What was the real, historical Bolívar like?

Physically, he was a small, slender man, energetic and impatient. People who knew him later disagreed about whether he was dark- or fair-skinned, but one thing everyone noticed was the intensity of his eyes.

He was an aristocrat, with the elegant manners and elaborate courtesy that came from being of one of Caracas's most privileged families. He retained his aristocratic manners all his life, even on the most difficult military campaigns when he and his men had only rags to wear.

He was exceptionally intelligent and, although his education had been spotty, very well read. He also spoke and wrote persuasively and elegantly, which can be seen from his eloquent speeches or any of the thousands of letters he wrote.

He was passionate—in both love and war. He often took actions that were rash and seemed to have no hope of success. Some of these actions resulted in brilliant victories, such as "The Amazing Campaign" of 1813, or the crossing of the Andes. But sometimes his passions led him to take actions that are harder to justify. One of these was arresting his commander-in-chief, Miranda, and turning him over to the Spaniards; another was the execution of Piar.

His passion for women, or perhaps his sense of chivalry, sometimes interfered with his passion for war. General Carlos Soublette, who was present at the patriot defeat at Ocumare, wrote (referring to Bolívar), "Into these events came love. . . . Marc Antony, unmindful of the danger in which he found himself, lost valuable time at Cleopatra's side."

In his biography of Bolívar, Gerhard Masur elaborates:

We know that Bolívar was never without a woman even in his war camps. Very likely he met his friend, Pepita, or another, in the port of Ocumare. Whether he was busy trying to rescue her, and thus, as Soublette says, lost valuable time, or whether she begged him to take her with him, will never be known.

His impulsiveness affected the way he governed after independence had been won. He assumed dictatorial powers in Gran Colombia and Peru, but used them inconsistently—some of the people he pardoned were real enemies; some of those he ordered executed probably were not. This is one reason there were so many conspiracies against him in his last years. Manuela Sáenz, the most memorable of his many women friends, saved his life one night in Bogotá, when his enemies came to assassinate him—she kept the conspirators busy while Bolívar escaped through a window, wearing her boots.

He died almost friendless, and bitter. Just five weeks before his death, he put down these pessimistic conclusions about the America he had liberated and the country, Gran Colombia, he had created:

1st, America is ungovernable by us; 2nd, whoever serves the revolution plows the sea; 3rd, the only thing that can be done in America is emigrate; 4th, this country will inevitably fall into the hands of an unbridled mob and then to the pettiest tyrants of every color and race; 5th, after we are devoured by all manner of crimes and extinguished by our own ferocity, the Europeans will not deign to conquer us; 6th, if it were possible for one part of the world to return to the primitive chaos, this would be the final period of America.

He had destroyed the world he knew—where good breeding was honored and lesser men accepted the rule of greater men—by destroying the colonial system, and he could not understand or accept the new world that he had helped create.

But this extraordinary man, the grand strategist of the independence of five nations, embodied a vision of a free, united country from Patagonia to the Río Grande that still inspires Latin Americans.

still dreaming of riding off to battle to bring his beloved Venezuela back into Colombia.

On December 17, 1830, at one P.M., he died. He was forty-seven years old. When the news reached Venezuela, there was cheering, with shouts of "The tyrant is dead!" The governor of Maracaibo rejoiced that Bolívar, "the spirit of evil, the author of all misfortunes, the oppressor of the fatherland," had died.

It would be many years before General Páez and his allies finally made their peace with Bolívar's ghost, turning him from "the spirit of evil" into the country's greatest hero. In 1846, the town of Angostura, from which Bolívar led his final, successful campaign to drive the Spaniards from South America, was renamed Ciudad Bolívar (Bolívar City).

Venezuela Independent: 1830–1908

The "Conservative Oligarchy" (1830–1847)

With Bolívar gone, the task of rebuilding the country after nearly twenty years of war fell to José Antonio Páez. The "Tiger of the Llanos" was now the undisputed supreme *caudillo*. He would dominate Venezuelan politics for the next eighteen years.

Páez had earned his nickname of "Tiger of the Llanos" for ferocious cavalry tactics during the war. *Caudillo* is an old Spanish word (from the Latin word *capitellum*, meaning "small head") for war chief, implying a man whose followers are loyal to him personally, no matter what reckless adventure he charges into. At the conclusion of the war, Vene-

José Antonio Páez, in an "ambrotype" (early form of photograph) by Federico Lessmann. Collection of the Birthplace of the Liberator, Caracas

zuela was full of *caudillos*, especially in the Llanos, and they would fight each other for most of the nineteenth century.

Bolívar had tried to be a different type of leader. He claimed his authority derived from his cause, liberty, and the patriot governments that had elected him, and he had not built up a large personal army—which is why, at the end, he died almost alone.

But with no stable government that could guarantee regular pay to the soldiers and no faith in the justice system, a personal army paid by the *caudillo* from his personal wealth or from booty was the only kind of army there could be. Mariño and Piar were *caudillos* who had been half tamed by Bolívar, so their armies were not entirely personal but could be put to the service of the larger war against Spain. But Páez had not been even half tamed.

Páez assumed the provisional presidency of Venezuela in May 1830—he did not even wait for Bolívar to die—and became the legal president under a new constitution the next year. Now his private army of *llaneros* could be paid out of the national treasury, an advantage for putting down revolts of other *caudillos*.

He also discovered that he enjoyed city life. And he realized that for Venezuela to develop, it needed Caracas. He filled his administration with wealthy, civilian *caraqueños* (people who lived in and around Caracas), who were the only people in the country sophisticated enough to deal with foreign bankers and merchants. This group became known as the "Conservative Oligarchy."

The oligarchy's wealth now came mainly from coffee rather than cacao. Many of the cacao plantations had been destroyed during the war, and the owners planted coffee instead. Coffee was selling for high prices on the world market in the 1830's, and a plant took less time than cacao to mature and produce fruit—five years, as compared to eight or ten for cacao. In the next few years, coffee cultivation would spread far beyond the old cacao-growing regions, up into the Andean valleys of

Trujillo, Mérida, and Táchira. Demand was high, and labor was in short supply. Slavery still existed, but since 1830, children of slaves had been born free, so the slave population was declining. To attract labor, planters had to offer wages that were higher than what a peasant could earn from farming on his own. As long as coffee prices remained high, all the coffee regions prospered. Most of the exports, however, still came from the valleys of Caracas and Aragua, just as they had for the *mantuanos* of colonial days.

The coffee boom restored the confidence of the Caracas elite, who made the mistake of thinking they could govern without Páez. The election of 1835 was won by their candidate, Dr. José María Vargas, a civilian who they thought would represent their interests. He defeated General Carlos Soublette, an independence hero loyal to Páez. Páez let Vargas take office and went back home to Apure, to wait.

He didn't have to wait long. Santiago Mariño and other independence-era generals, thinking Páez was on their side, overthrew Vargas in the "Revolution of the Reforms," demanding constitutional changes and rewards for their war services. But Páez brought his lancers up from the Llanos and destroyed the revolution, and brought Vargas back to the presidential chair. However, when Páez would not let him punish the leaders of the revolt, Vargas gave up pretending to govern, and in 1836 he resigned. Páez's ally Soublette filled out the term. Páez returned to govern personally from 1839 to 1843, and Soublette for the term 1843–1847.

Two Venezuelas

There were really two Venezuelas, as different as two worlds, but neither could live without the other.

One was the sophisticated world of the cities, especially Caracas, where there was a class of educated, wealthy people who went to church

Caracas in 1853, as viewed from the top of El Calvario Hill by the British artist Joseph Thomas.   Collection of the Venezuelan National Library

and debating clubs and concerts, rode through the city and to their country estates in handsome carriages, lived in large, open houses surrounded by gardens cultivated by their servants. When they traveled abroad, they preferred Paris, and some of them spoke very good French and knew Paris as well as, or even better than, Caracas. In this class were the people who understood about banking and trade.

The city also included other people, most of them *pardos* or free blacks, who worked in small businesses or workshops or sold goods on the street. Finally, there were black slaves, working as servants or laborers. Although all children of slaves born after 1830 by law were free, their parents would not be freed until 1854. But whatever their color or status, all these people were familiar with city ways.

The other Venezuela was the rough countryside, where city ways were useless. Especially in the Llanos, violence substituted for the rule of law. Here were the *caudillos*, cattlemen who could raise an army from their cowhands and all the local people who owed them favors, and could defy the authority of Caracas.

There were also groups of bandits roaming the plains, hunting cattle and assaulting travelers. Since the war these groups, made up mostly of veterans, had become more numerous and more dangerous. When leather prices went up in Europe, they simply killed and skinned cattle, leaving the meat for the buzzards and selling the hides in San Fernando or Angostura. Nobody's herd was safe.

One woman grinds corn while another prepares casabe, *a flatbread made from the ground root of the yucca plant. From* Wild Scenes in South America, or Life in the Llanos of Venezuela, *by Ramón Páez, New York, 1862.*

"Law of the Lashes"

They didn't think of themselves as rustlers, because they didn't accept that anybody could "own" cattle—if the animals were there on the plains, anybody who could catch them could have them. Páez had attempted to control this theft by setting up roving bands of police and imposing stricter penalties, including whippings of rustlers. But the mounted police squads were ineffective against the *llaneros*, and the "Ley de Azotes" (Law of Lashes) enraged them so much that they killed the first judge who tried to apply it and rose in revolt in 1837.

The cultured civilians in Caracas could not govern without the support of the wilder *caudillos*, but the *caudillos* also needed Caracas. For one thing, they wanted the imported goods that made their lives more splendid and their power more extensive—fancy saddles and new guns, for example. For another, as Páez recognized, governing from Caracas was the only way a *caudillo* could have power outside his own region.

Great Britain, France, and the other foreign countries that lent the planters and ranchers money and bought their products did not much care what happened outside Caracas, just as long as payments were kept up and orders for coffee and hides were fulfilled. They considered Caracas rather quaint and pleasant; the rest of the country they saw as grotesquely barbarous, the setting for bad novels and vaudeville skits. This attitude would prevail for over a century.

Godos and Debtors

In the early 1840's, the fall of coffee prices split the elite into two factions: those who owed money, and those to whom it was owed. In 1834, wanting to please foreign investors and having no idea what the consequences might be, Congress passed a law eliminating the old Spanish colonial limits on interest rates and permitting a debtor's goods to be auctioned to satisfy his creditors. During the coffee boom, most planters had borrowed heavily at high interest, to expand production. Now, unable to pay the loans, many of them were losing everything in auctions.

The group around Páez included merchants, moneylenders, and the agents of foreign bankers. They called themselves Conservatives, but their opponents called them *godos* (Goths), an independence-era insult for the Spaniards. The other group called themselves Liberals, and demanded policies that would be more favorable to debtors. But the importance of this ideological split should not be exaggerated. In practice, whether one lined up with one party or the other usually had more to do with old family and regional alliances and feuds than with any substantive policy difference.

The Liberal opposition to Páez was organized by the party founder, Antonio Leocadio Guzmán, a skillful propagandist who also played upon the grievances of the *llaneros*.

In 1846, two *llanero* chieftains, Francisco José Rangel and Ezequiel Zamora, led an especially serious revolt against the government, shouting Liberal party slogans. Many of these rebels were *pardos*, bent on ridding the country of all whites—which was no part of Guzmán's plan and scared the wits out of all the whites. The rebellion failed, however, and the government of President Soublette arrested Guzmán and sentenced him to death for treason.

The "Liberal Oligarchy" of the Monagas Brothers (1847–1857)

In 1847, Páez chose another independence veteran, General José Tadeo Monagas, as his candidate for president—which assured his election. But Monagas brought Liberals into his government and, defying Páez and the Conservatives, commuted Guzmán's death sentence to one of exile. Páez then attempted to overthrow him. But the old Tiger of the Llanos had lost touch with the new generation of *llaneros*, and too few of them answered his call to arms for him to do the job. Defeated and briefly imprisoned, Páez left for the Caribbean and later New York.

The Monagas government is often called the "Liberal Oligarchy," because Guzmán's Liberal Party at first had influence. But after neutralizing the Conservatives—even letting a mob attack them in Congress—Monagas soon shoved Guzmán aside as well, and chose his own brother, General José Gregorio Monagas (also an independence veteran), to succeed him in rigged elections.

In the long run, this was probably just as well for Guzmán. During the Monagas years, world coffee prices were down and interest rates high, leaving the planter class with debts they couldn't pay. With too little money coming in either to satisfy its rivals or to eliminate them, the government faced increasingly serious revolts from both Liberals *and* Conservatives.

To eliminate one source of contention, the possibility of slave uprisings, President José Gregorio Monagas and Congress abolished slavery in 1854. Some die-hard slaveowners were so furious, they gave their slaves beatings before freeing them; but once freed, the ex-slaves took their revenge. However, neither José Gregorio nor his brother, who returned to the presidency in 1856, was able to repress the growing banditry and rebelliousness of the *caudillos* of the Llanos.

Castro to Guzmán Blanco (1857–1870)

In 1857, when José Tadeo Monagas rammed through Congress a new constitution permitting him to be reelected, his enemies, led by Julián Castro, governor of Carabobo, overthrew him, and Monagas took refuge in the French Legation (embassy). His removal from power unleashed a struggle for power in twelve years of civil wars, between the "Federalists," who wanted more power for their home regions, and the "Conservatives" based in Caracas.

First, Juan Crisóstomo Falcón, a Liberal from Coro, taking advantage of a blockade of the port by France and Great Britain, invaded at La Guaira. When the invasion failed, Falcón went into exile, along with Ezequiel Zamora, who had led the revolt against Páez twelve years earlier.

They soon were back with their new slogan of "Federalism," trying to overthrow Conservatives Pedro Gual and then Manuel Felipe Tovar, who took over from Castro in 1859. The first of the Federal Wars ended when Zamora was assassinated and, later, his forces were defeated at Coplé in 1860.

Páez seized this moment to return from his exile in New York. His arrival in 1861 caused Conservatives Tovar and Gual to split, and Páez took command of the Conservative forces. But in 1863, the Federalists, led by Falcón, finally won their war, ended by the Treaty of Coche. Páez returned to New York, where he wrote an eloquent *Autobiography* and lived out the rest of his long life, dying peacefully in 1873.

Falcón became president. His vice president was General Antonio Guzmán Blanco (1829–1899), son of the Liberal propagandist Antonio Leocadio Guzmán.

Although the Federal Wars were supposedly over, revolts—or "revolutions," as they were called—continued against the Federalist government. Finally old General José Tadeo Monagas, now eighty-two, took charge of a coalition of Liberals and Conservatives and drove the government from Caracas. Falcón went into exile in Curaçao, close to his home region of Coro, where he died the next year; the state of Falcón is now named for him.

Monagas was all set to be president once again, but he died, and Congress named his son, General José Ruperto Monagas, as president

Too Many Generals

One reason there were so many revolutions, suggests Venezuelan historian Guillermo Morón, was that so many men depended on war to make a living. He found, from the Census of 1873, that "the State of Carabobo alone had 449 generals, 627 colonels, 967 majors, 818 captains, 504 lieutenants and eighty-five second lieutenants—no less than 3,450 commissioned officers. The male population over twenty-one years of age was 22,952; which means that in that State over 15 percent of the active men were army officers. If this figure is applied to the whole country it will be easy to understand why there were revolutions."

In a letter home about one of the many revolutions in the 1880's, the U.S. Minister (which is what ambassadors were called in those days) wrote, "They are fighting from time to time in La Guaira in preparation for a greater fight—like olives before dinner. . . . Nobody knows what it is about, but peace makes them uneasy."

For the officers, it was all glorious, and fighting gave them the chance to advance their careers. Not so for their men.

in 1868. This was when Antonio Guzmán Blanco, in command of the Federalist and Liberal opposition, led an invasion from Coro and, after a three-day siege, occupied Caracas in April 1870.

The Rule of Guzmán Blanco (1870–1888)

Antonio Guzmán Blanco (1829–1899) had learned politics and propaganda from his father, the Liberal firebrand Antonio Leocadio Guzmán.

Soldiers were recruited by force. A general would say, "I need so many men by such-and-such a time," and patrols would go out to grab them from their homes, the marketplace, walking along mountain trails, coming out of theaters, or anywhere. T. R. Ybarra, who was a child at the time, describes seeing "long lines of men in rags. They were black with dirt. Dirty ropes tied them together, two by two. They were escorted by officers with drawn swords or machetes, and soldiers with muskets. The faces of the roped men were gray with fatigue. Their cheeks were hollow, their eyes sunken, their gait stumbling. Many of them were listlessly sucking oranges. Orange peels littered the cobblestones around them." These recruits would receive thirty centavos a day and very little training. "If they did not perish in battle, or rot from disease, they could hope to go home after two or three years—unless their officers were too busy to bother about the trifling fact that they had served their time." The lucky ones might get assigned as orderlies to officers. Unlucky ones might be wounded in some skirmish and be left on the battlefield to die—some military wives tried to create an ambulance corps, but without much success.

He had become a general at the side of Falcón and Zamora during the Federal Wars, and Falcón's vice president in the 1860's; he developed his own following in the Federalist and Liberal movements (the Liberals at this time were divided, some with Guzmán and the Federalists and some with the Conservatives). He was a natural leader of the opposition to José Ruperto Monagas, and his military seizure of Caracas at the head of eight thousand men assured his dominance of the country.

Guzmán impressed his contemporaries as a very handsome man, with elegant manners. A sign that he was a true aristocrat was that, like

Double Surnames

Antonio Guzmán Blanco's mother was related to the Bolívars—which is no doubt why he added her family name, "Blanco," after "Guzmán." In double surnames, the mother's is in most cases considered a kind of adornment, and it would be an error to call someone by it; the "real" family name, the one passed on to one's children, is the surname of the father. Thus Guzmán Blanco might be called "Guzmán," but never "Blanco." The period of his government, 1870 to 1888, is commonly called the "Guzmanato" (rule of Guzmán).

Other prominent Venezuelans who have chosen to use a double surname include the early twentieth-century historian Laureano VALLENILLA Lanz, the contemporary writer Luis BRITTO García, and several presidents, including Marcos PÉREZ Jiménez (1952–1958) and Luis HERRERA Campins (1979–1984).

Bolívar, he had tiny feet—he could wear his wife's slippers (oddly, small feet were not especially praised in women).

He was an intelligent and skillful politician, knowing how to play off the urban and rustic chiefs against one another. His chief aim as president was to bring Venezuela into the modern, urban world, so that it would be a more nearly equal partner of the developed Atlantic nations he admired—and especially France, which he loved.

His first problem was achieving peace: there were seventy-eight "actions of war" in the country in his first year in office, and thirty-nine the next. He achieved peace, gradually, by defeating some rebels and coming to arrangements with other *caudillos*: Each was permitted to run

Antonio Guzmán Blanco strikes a heroic pose on this visiting card produced by A. Pearsall. The white horse, which also appears on the national shield, is a traditional symbol of power in Venezuela.
Miraflores Archives

his region however he liked, as long as he kept public order. In return, the federal government would give grants of money to the region and, if necessary, send federal troops to help him against local rivals.

But, apart from his skill, what made Guzmán's whole long rule possible was something over which neither he nor any other Venezuelan had any control: The early 1880's were boom times in the world market, with high prices for coffee, cacao, and cattle, and plenty of foreign capital interested in investing in agriculture, railroads, and public works. This inflow of capital enabled Guzmán to satisfy the demands of the various groups he had to hold together to stay in power. It also enabled him to steal from the public treasury on a much grander scale than any of his predecessors, by developing what was—for Venezuela—a new technique: Taking a large cut for himself from loans and foreign contracts. He also used his presidential power to acquire lands that came up for auction. All in all, he became a very wealthy man.

In an attempt to make Caracas into the Paris of South America, Guzmán installed new wide boulevards and huge public buildings, *plazas*, and statuary; provided the capital with water, sewers, and electrical services; and improved on public transportation. The railroad between Caracas and La Guaira, which Richard Harding Davis was to describe in 1896, was completed in 1883. An exceedingly vain man, Guzmán Blanco put his name on the handsome new buildings and erected statues to himself all over the city. He liked to be called "El Ilustre Americano" (The Illustrious American) and he had the state of Bolívar, the former province of Caracas, renamed "Guzmán Blanco."

Guzmán's legacy also included the first telegraph links between Caracas and the rest of the country (a line between Caracas and La Guaira had been inaugurated in 1856) and the modernization of the army, with more professional organization and better weapons. These would change the character of regional revolts in the future.

As long as the boom continued, Guzmán managed to spend long periods in Europe, his hotel and entertainment bills being paid at huge expense by the national treasury. Meanwhile he would leave someone else governing in his stead for a two-year presidential term. When he was bored with Europe, or worried about changes back home, he would return and resume power. But in 1884, just as one of his substitutes, Joaquín Crespo, was assuming office, a world economic crisis caught up with Venezuela. When he returned in 1886, he met greater opposition and his government became more repressive.

Finally, in 1888, he left for good. Under the man he had urged Congress to elect in his place, Juan Pablo Rojas Paúl, a strong anti–Guzmán Blanco reaction began. Mobs tore down his statues, and his name was taken off all the things he had named for himself. In 1889 the state of Guzmán Blanco was renamed Miranda, which is still its name today.

From Guzmán to Gómez (1888–1908)

With Guzmán Blanco gone and coffee prices down again, the next few years were turbulent, with several changes of government. In 1892, General Joaquín Crespo, who had been president in one of the periods that Guzmán was out of the country (1884–1886), seized power in what he called the "Legalist Revolution." The economic crisis had thrown many people out of work, and in 1895 Caracas saw its first massive labor protest, by three thousand workers and artisans. That year there were also protests against Great Britain, for its claims against territory in the Guayana. The first Congress of Workers met in 1896 to form a Popular Party, advocating better workers' education and the establishment of workers cooperatives.

In 1899, General Cipriano Castro, a *caudillo* from Táchira in the Andes, raised an army and came to power at the head of the "Liberal Restoration Revolution." T. R. Ybarra watched his entry into Caracas.

He came into the city at the head of thousands of pallid and sinewy soldiers, brandishing *peinillas*, the cruel curved blades that are the counterpart, in the Andean regions of Venezuela, of the machete of the rest of the republic. In their ranks, as they surged through the streets of the capital, were many women, also armed with *peinillas* and carbines and revolvers; I remember well standing on the sidelines of Castro's parade of victory and seeing the unkempt and muddy wenches of his soldiery waving their weapons over their heads, amid uninhibited whoops of triumph.

Castro would be the first of a long succession of strong men from Táchira. His government, corrupt and hard-pressed for money because of the economic crisis, ignored foreign creditors' demands for payment

City and Country in the 1890's

T. R. Ybarra, a Venezuelan-American journalist who wrote for U.S. publications, has left a vivid memoir of his youth in Venezuela in the 1890's, *Young Man of Caracas*. In those days little horse-drawn streetcars, with seats for twelve and standing room for about ten more, clip-clopped up the hills to the outlying neighborhoods from the Plaza Bolívar. Peddlers sold bread rolls from barrels strapped to the sides of little donkeys. Furniture moving was done by muscular *parihueleros* (litter bearers) who loaded the goods on a wooden trestle, secured with heavy ropes running from the handles across the bearers' shoulders, backs, and necks, and trotted through the city with everything from chairs to pianos.

The houses, all with red tile roofs, were painted in various colors, and were almost all single-story, because of fear of earthquakes. Closed to the street, they opened to an inner patio that provided fresh air and had decorative plants and, often, a variety of family pets—the Ybarra household had a deer, an egret, a cat, and a very loud parrot that wandered around freely, sometimes startling their foreign guests. Dropping in unexpectedly for lunch was quite normal—the cook, often a servant who probably had brought her children, cousins, or other family members into the household, would always have prepared plenty of fried plantains, black beans, and meat for everybody.

An uncle of Ybarra's had a coffee plantation in Turgua, a hilly, forested area now about a two-hour drive south from Caracas, but then reachable by a little English-owned train. (Trains have practically disappeared from Venezuela, which now relies on road and air transport almost exclusively.) "Little shacks hugged the

From the interior patio of a nineteenth-century house in La Pastora, a neighborhood of Caracas; the "Drink Coca-Cola" garbage-can lid is a later addition. Vladimir Sersa

steep mountainsides. They were roofed with big yellowing leaves and walled with sheets of tin, beaten out flat, which had begun life as American kerosene cans." One of the boy's great pleasures was diving headfirst into the piles of millions of the greenish coffee berries—at the risk of picking up the nasty little insects, *niguas* and *garrapatas*, that burrow under the skin and are hard to dig out. Another pleasure was a *joropo*, a country dance held by the coffee pickers, which would really get exciting after the plantation owner and his wife, as the guests of honor, had had the first dance.

of debts, and European interests financed an attempt to overthrow him. When that failed, English, German, and Italian warships blockaded the Venezuelan ports in 1902. This dispute was settled with the intervention of the United States: by the Washington Protocol, Venezuela had to allocate 30 percent of its customs duties—the main source of legal revenue—to paying the European debts.

Castro had no great political skill or even interest in government affairs, but he did improve the telegraph network, build a few more miles of railroad in the central and coastal region, and improve the weaponry of the army—all because his chief interests were military. His government was disorderly, disreputable, and colorful. Its chief importance in Venezuelan history is that it was the vehicle for achieving power of Castro's right hand man, his vice president and finally his betrayer: Juan Vicente Gómez.

Cipriano Castro's health had begun to deteriorate—too much brandy and too many women, according to Ybarra—and in 1908 he left for medical treatments in Germany. His vice president, Juan Vicente Gómez, permitted—or instigated—an anti-Castro demonstration, and then, on December 19, took over the presidency. He had pulled off one of the smoothest coups in the country's history. He would run the country for twenty-seven years, and would bring it into the modern world.

President Cipriano Castro, seated, with his Minister of War, Juan Vicente Gómez, behind him, shortly before Gómez deposed his boss. Collection of the Venezuelan National Library

The Modern State: 1908 to Today

Dictatorship of Juan Vicente Gómez (1908–1935)

Juan Vicente Gómez was a shrewd but uncultured man, even less adapted to city life than Cipriano Castro. For most of his long rule, he governed from a ranch he acquired in Maracay, requiring senators and others who needed to see him to travel several hours by train or car west from Caracas. He had himself proclaimed *"El Benemérito"* ("The Meritorious"), but behind his back he was called *"El Bagre"* ("The Catfish"). This was partly because of his big whiskers and also, perhaps, because he said very little and swallowed up property the way a catfish swallows up everything on the bottom of a stream.

Like Castro, Gómez was from the high mountain state of Táchira. He was a cattleman who had rarely left the Andean valleys until 1899, when he was about forty-two, and joined Castro's revolution. As ruler of Venezuela, he made himself the country's biggest landowner and

*Juan Vicente Gómez
as president.* Luis F. Toro,
Collection of the Venezuelan
National Library

cattle rancher. He forced ranchers to sell to him at ridiculous prices or simply seized their property.

He could barely read, and didn't see much use for it. He brooked no dissent, and did not care the least about public opinion—especially the opinion of educated city people. He sent their sons to prison when they protested his policies.

What he was most notorious for, both in Venezuela and abroad, was institutionalized rape. When he saw a woman who attracted him, he would signal an aide. Army officers would then approach the woman, threatening or bribing her father or husband if necessary, and bring her to his bed. If he was pleased with her, he rewarded her and her family. It was said that Gómez, who never married, fathered over one hundred children, a few of whom he brought up in his household. He is the principal model for the monster-dictator in Gabriel García Márquez's novel *The Autumn of the Patriarch*.

Peace and Petroleum

Crude and ignorant as he was, Gómez accomplished two things that would transform Venezuela forever. First, he brought twenty-seven years of governmental stability, the longest peace since independence. Second, he encouraged the exploitation of petroleum.

To achieve peace, Gómez modernized the army, improving its professional training, weaponry, and communications. He filled the top ranks with loyal officers from his native Táchira. This gave him such an enormous advantage over his opponents that he easily squashed revolts of the type that had destabilized every government since independence. He rewarded his favorite officers with high pay and ranches. When military men were discovered conspiring against him, which first happened on a large scale in 1919, he had them and their civilian allies imprisoned and tortured mercilessly.

He also had the good luck to be in power when the oil boom started. Automobiles were beginning to replace horse-drawn vehicles, and the new airplanes, ships, and other vehicles would all need gasoline. In 1914, the Caribbean Petroleum Company, a subsidiary of Royal Dutch Shell, began producing oil from a well on the shore of Lake Maracaibo, and by 1917 petroleum exports began.

Gómez granted the foreign companies the right to drill and export oil in return for payments to his government. Today, looking back at these concessions, Gómez looks very foolish for giving away the oil so cheaply. But at the time, any payment for oil seemed to most Venezuelans like free money, because it didn't require any effort on their part and wasn't taking away anything the country had ever used. Before, nobody had wanted the sticky black stuff oozing out of the ground, and Venezuela had lots of it.

The results of the exploitation of oil by Royal Dutch Shell, Standard Oil of New Jersey (the forerunner of Exxon), and other foreign companies were threefold. First, the sale of concessions gave the Gómez government the money it needed to pay off its military officers and other allies and to build some public works (since the government used convict labor for road building, these were pretty cheap in any case).

Second, oil production greatly increased the involvement of foreigners in the national economy, especially "Americans"—as Venezuelans learned to call people from the United States. These foreign companies grew to be giants, in part from their profits on Venezuelan oil, and their power was felt in several ways. They could easily corrupt the local police and justice system, for example, to protect their interests in labor disputes. With a little more expense, they could corrupt top government officials as well, to get even more concessions—tax breaks, bargains on other property, army and police protection, and exemptions from health and safety laws. This foreign influence was especially obvious in the area around Lake Maracaibo, where there were whole towns completely run by the oil companies. It built up popular resentment against the foreigners, especially Americans, that would have serious repercussions after Gómez's death.

The third major result of the oil boom in Venezuela was a social transformation. The country rapidly became more urban and industrial and less agricultural, as small farmers and peons (landless laborers) left the land to become oil workers in the new company towns. The class of white-collar, administrative employees also grew rapidly. Workers began organizing into unions, over the very strong and brutal opposition of the companies and the governments, while the middle class sought to create new political organizations to express their demands.

Strike!
These changes created strong tensions, and a 1928 strike by university and high-school students led to riots and an attempted revolt against the government by young military officers. Gómez cracked down very hard, arresting and torturing hundreds of suspects. Seventeen- and eighteen-year-old students were sent to the damp, dark

Gómez's many enemies called him El Bagre *("The Catfish"). This caricature of* El Bagre *appeared in print just 48 hours after his death. From* Gómez: Tyrant of the Andes, *by Thomas Rourke.*

dungeons of the old Spanish castle of Puerto Cabello and other prisons, where they were barely fed and were forced to do hard labor while wearing heavy leg irons that chafed and tore the flesh of their legs. Gómez also shut down the Central University of Venezuela, center of the protests. The survivors of that student revolt would call themselves "The Generation of 1928," and would include Venezuela's most important political leaders in the years to come.

The next year, there were more rebellions across the country, but Gómez's loyal forces managed to defeat them all. Also in 1929, Venezuela became the world's largest oil exporter. Venezuela would therefore survive the world-wide depression that began that year much better than most countries. The only thing now that could defeat Gómez was old age. He died quietly in his bed in 1935, at age seventy-eight. He had always claimed that his birthday was September 24, the same as Simón Bolívar's, and somehow he managed to die on December 17, the same date as the death of his beloved Liberator.

At Gómez's death, fourteen tons of leg irons, some weighing seventy-five pounds, were thrown into the sea at the base of the prison in Puerto Cabello. The cruel thugs and secret police of the regime now had to flee from angry mobs. The professional army, which had held itself apart from the Gómez clan's greatest excesses, turned power over to Gómez's Minister of War and the Navy, General Eleazar López Contreras, age fifty-two, who was also from the state of Táchira.

Populist Reforms: First Attempts (1936–1945)

López Contreras was very conservative, but he was far more flexible than Gómez and more sensitive to both local and international opinion. Exiles from the Gómez years, including members of the Generation of 1928, returned and began organizing political parties and labor unions. In 1936, several leftist groups joined together in the PDN or Partido Democrático Nacional (Democratic National Party), forerunner of Acción Democrática (Democratic Action), which is today the most powerful party in the country.

Venezuela was now an urban society with modern communications and a professional army. The feuds between the Liberal and Conservative Parties, which had dominated politics before Gómez, were now completely irrelevant, and the *caudillo* tradition that had brought Gómez to power was almost dead—a rancher could no longer gather his peons, issue a call to arms, and march on the capital. The new leaders did not think of the country as a giant private ranch dependent mainly on cattle raising and cultivation by ignorant and obedient peons. Instead, they wanted to use the great oil wealth to create a modern, urban society with advanced technology and customs, comparable to New York, Paris, or Miami.

President Isaías Medina Angarita and his wife at an official gathering. P. A. Manrique, collection of P. J. Manrique

When López's term was up in 1941, he nominated his Minister of War and the Navy, General Isaías Medina Angarita, to be elected by Congress as his successor. The novelist Rómulo Gallegos, of the party Acción Democrática, dared to run against him, getting 13 votes against Medina's 120.

Medina had been listening to his opponents and began enacting reforms of the type they proposed. His government increased Venezuela's share of petroleum revenue to 30 percent and created an income tax, social security, and an agrarian reform law to distribute government land to peasants. But the young activists of Acción Democrática, led by Rómulo Betancourt, were impatient to end military rule forever. And the way they did it, ironically enough, was by promoting a military coup.

The *"Trienio"* (1945–1948)

In October 1945, a group of young officers calling themselves the Military Patriotic Union, aided by AD (Acción Democrática), overthrew the government of General Isaías Medina Angarita and sent him and López Contreras into exile. They created a military-civilian *junta*, with AD leader Rómulo Betancourt as its president. AD would be in power for a period of three years—in Spanish, a *trienio*.

The *junta* headed by Betancourt repealed Medina's agrarian reform law and raised Venezuela's share of the oil income to 50 percent. The military, however, was almost entirely excluded from these decisions, and was growing resentful. They also were worried about AD's revolutionary rhetoric.

In 1947, the AD candidate, the country's best-known writer, Rómulo Gallegos, became the first president by popular election—that is, elected directly by the citizens and not by Congress or any other special body. He took office in February 1948. By now, however, the officers who had supported the 1945 coup were extremely nervous about the rapid pace of change and AD's failure to consult them. In November 1948, they deposed him and took over the government themselves.

A Military Interruption (1948–1958)

The new *junta* was made up of three lieutenant colonels: Carlos Delgado Chalbaud, president of the *junta*; Marcos Pérez Jiménez; and Luis

A Trio of Leaders: Betancourt, Villalba, Caldera

Rómulo Betancourt (1908–1982) was one of a trio of highly talented politicians from the Generation of 1928, who built political parties around their personalities. The others were Jóvito Villalba, who founded the Unión Republicana Democrática, or URD (Democratic Republican Union), and Rafael Caldera, who created a social Catholic party known by its initials, COPEI (for Comité para la Organización Política y Elección Independiente, or Committee for Political Organization and Independent Election).

Of the three, Betancourt was by far the most successful party builder. He had briefly joined the Communist Party while he was in exile in Costa Rica and had picked up some Marxist terminology, which would become part of AD's early platforms. But once he got back to Venezuela, Betancourt turned out to be the Communists' most tenacious opponent.

Short, pudgy, and generally unattractive physically—his opponents often drew him as a frog—he was nevertheless capable of giving spellbinding speeches, using strange words (some of them

Felipe Llovera Páez. They quickly outlawed AD, disbanded the Confederación de Trabajadores Venezolanos (Venezuelan Workers Federation), or CTV, suspended classes at the Central University, and outlawed the Communist Party. When Delgado Chalbaud was assassinated in November 1950, a civilian was temporarily put into office, but the real power was held by Pérez Jiménez, another military chief from the Andean state of Táchira, where he was born in 1914.

invented by himself) that left his peasant listeners in awe. More importantly, he had a keen sense of his opponents' weaknesses and was quite prepared to make whatever alliances were necessary to achieve power for his party. In the 1945 coup, he sensed that General Medina could be forced out of office, but only if the military did the pushing. The greatest strength of Betancourt's party was in the oil workers' union, but he was also keen on building support among peasants and the middle class.

Villalba's supporters were mainly from the urban middle class, which turned out not to be a base large enough for him to achieve supreme power. A slender, prematurely bald man who had been one of the most fiery leaders of the university revolt of 1928, he was an effective orator but not much of an organizer, and his party's strength depended almost entirely on his personal popularity.

Caldera, an elegant, black-haired man who had been only 12 years old in 1928, was also an effective speaker. He built a strong party, COPEI, which in later years would win the presidency twice, the first time with Caldera. His problem was that not enough Venezuelans felt strongly enough about being Catholic to support him for that reason, and Betancourt and the AD out-organized him with the unions and peasant groups.

In the elections of 1952, URD candidate Jóvito Villalba—free from competition by AD or the Communists—appeared to be winning against the government candidate, Pérez Jiménez. "P.J.," as he was called, stopped the count and declared himself the winner. Villalba was put on a plane leaving the country.

Marcos Pérez Jiménez was nearly as vain as Antonio Guzmán Blanco, but not half as smart. He promoted himself to general and strutted around in elaborate uniforms. He built a huge housing complex for his officers and named it for the date on which he had seized power, the Second of December (1952). He also accumulated so many medals, the list filled half a column in a newspaper—including the United States' Legion of Merit, pinned to his white uniform by President Dwight David Eisenhower in 1954.

He called his governmental program the "New National Ideal," which came down to massive public works and heavy repression. He used the country's oil money to build an impressive network of super-highways, including a cloverleaf interchange so complicated that *caraqueños* call it "The Octopus." Another of his projects was building the Hotel Humboldt on top of Mount Avila, accessible only by cablecar; the cablecar is broken so much of the time that the hotel, with its

Portrait of noted novelist and president of Venezuela Rómulo Gallegos.

magnificent view, has only rarely been used. He also ordered construction of hydroelectric dams and a massive spiral structure in Caracas known as the "Helicoide," intended to hold shopping centers, offices, and housing; it was never completed, but the shell stands as a monument to the regime's wastefulness.

There was nothing modern about the repression, however. Pérez Jiménez's opponents were seized by the secret police, the Seguridad Nacional, and tortured as brutally and in as primitive ways as in the days of Gómez or Guzmán Blanco. The Communists, AD, and—after Villalba was exiled—the URD were all conspiring against him, and opposition was very strong in the unions and the universities. Even the armed forces had become disgusted with his arbitrary ways.

On January 23, 1958, these opposition forces came together in a three-day general strike that paralyzed Caracas at the same time as a rebellion by the air force. Pérez Jiménez rushed to the airport and took off for exile in Miami. Angry mobs stormed the offices of the Seguridad Nacional, looking for the torturers and destroying the buildings. The housing complex built for his officers was taken over by civilians and given a new name: the Twenty-Third of January.

Emergency Plan of 1958

A new civilian-military *junta* now took command, under Rear Admiral Wolfgang Larrazábal, aged forty-seven, to organize a national election to restore democratic government. The *junta* abolished the hated Seguridad Nacional and declared an "Emergency Plan," calling for government compensation for unemployed workers and public works for poor neighborhoods. Political activists who had been in the underground now organized takeovers of vacant land by the homeless, who then pressured the government for water and other services.

Left- and right-wing groups continued to agitate. Rightists in the army tried to depose Larrazábal several times, and actually seized power for a few hours. But the civilian population of Caracas immediately declared a general strike that paralyzed the city, and the mutineers resigned.

In May, Communist sympathizers and unemployed workers disrupted a visit by U.S. Vice President Richard M. Nixon to Caracas, threatening his life when his car was stopped by a mob. The support that the United States had given to Pérez Jiménez was still on everybody's mind, and Americans were also deeply resented for the high-handed policies of the oil companies.

In the elections in November 1958, Larrazábal ran for president as the candidate of the URD, with support from the Communists. Although he carried Caracas, he was defeated by Rómulo Betancourt of Acción Democrática, who had a much more efficient organization nationwide.

The Betancourt Administration (1959–1964)

With the inauguration of Rómulo Betancourt as president, freely elected by the people, Venezuela at last entered the era of stable, multiparty democracy that continues today. But after all the turmoil of the previous years, it would not be easy. Betancourt would have to use his considerable political skill to balance, appease, or suppress the many groups making conflicting demands.

In the first year of Betancourt's government, there were attempted uprisings by the right-wingers, loyal to Pérez Jiménez and aided by the dictator of the Dominican Republic, Rafael Leonidas Trujillo. In 1962, left-wing units of the National Guard and Marine Corps revolted in Carúpano, and another Marine Corps battalion revolted in Puerto Cabello; both risings were put down bloodily.

The back cover of the underground Communist newspaper Tribuna Popular *for June 1, 1963, denounces U.S. President John F. Kennedy for sending missiles, and Rómulo Betancourt for using them, against the Venezuelan Marine Corps mutiny in Puerto Cabello.*

Guerrilla War

The success of the Cuban revolution on January 1, 1959, thrilled many young workers and students in Venezuela, who were already resentful of the United States. In 1960, a group of AD militants split from the party to form the Movimiento de la Izquierda Revolucionaria, or MIR (Movement of the Revolutionary Left). They soon forged an alliance with the Communist Party and some nationalist army and navy officers to create the Fuerzas Armadas de Liberación Nacional, or FALN (Armed Forces of National Liberation).

The FALN carried out many spectacular attacks, including the hijacking of an ocean freighter on the high seas and an airplane in midflight (the first political air hijacking in history), the theft of Impressionist paintings from an exhibit in Caracas, blowing up of pipelines, and kidnappings, including a Spanish soccer star and, at different times, two U.S. military attachés. Normally the urban operations were carried out by small squads of four to eight combatants, frequently including women, for lightning raids. Their uniforms were like those of the army, but with FALN insignia.

The FALN also attempted to set up "liberated zones" in the countryside, following the Cuban model. However, Venezuela had changed too much for a rural revolt to work. Too many peasants had moved to the cities, and many of the others supported the government party, AD, which promised land reform. During most of the years the FALN maintained its struggle, the rural *guerrillas* found very little support and depended almost entirely on their comrades in the city for supplies.

The FALN never developed a mass base in the cities, either—its members were mostly university students, with few workers and even fewer peasants. The organization struggled on for several

Guerrilla commander Douglas Bravo (foreground) with another guerrilla identified as Mariño, from the underground publication El Patriota, *July 9, 1963.*

years, suffering many casualties without gaining wider support. The Communist Party finally abandoned the armed struggle in 1965, and was legalized in 1969. One famous *guerrilla* chieftain, Douglas Bravo, continued fighting in the state of Falcón into the 1970's. His group was isolated, however, and depended heavily on his family connections throughout the area—much like the *caudillos* of the past century.

The survivors of this whole bloody, violent saga have since been integrated into the legal political process. Revolutionary politics are no longer on the agenda of any major group in Venezuela.

Unionized workers were demanding a larger share of the nation's oil wealth. The Communist party had considerable union support, because of its resistance to Pérez Jiménez and because of effective organizing. Betancourt's party, Acción Democrática, whose members had also fought courageously against the dictatorship, competed with the Communists for control.

To fulfill campaign promises and keep his supporters, Betancourt needed to increase Venezuela's share of the wealth from oil exploitation, but he was not prepared to nationalize production as some of the other parties were demanding. The United States was Venezuela's best customer for its oil, and U.S. companies owned most of the business. The overthrow of a reformist government in Guatemala in 1954 by the Central Intelligence Agency demonstrated how far the United States was willing to go to defend its property interests.

Betancourt's policies could not have satisfied everybody, and the left wing of his party was particularly dissatisfied with the slow progress of agrarian reform and the apparent subservience to U.S. interests. After dealing with his right-wing opponents, Betancourt was confronted by a revolutionary *guerrilla* movement inspired by the Cuban revolution.

Achieving Political Stability (1964–1973)

In 1963, the FALN made an all-out effort to disrupt the election of Betancourt's successor. The *guerrillas* failed. Protected by the massive deployment of army and police forces, voters went to the polls and elected Dr. Raúl Leoni, the candidate of Acción Democrática, with 33 percent of the votes.

Since then, Venezuelan politics have been very stable, with fairly peaceful, multiparty, democratic elections for president every five years. AD remains the most powerful party, and has won every presidential election but two, when it lost to COPEI: in 1969, under COPEI's founder, Rafael Caldera, and 1979, with Luis Herrera Campins. The URD has dwindled to become a minor force, its place as the third party being taken by the Movimiento al Socialismo or MAS (Movement Toward Socialism), which was founded by former *guerrillas.* This is a reformist, left-of-center party, which holds several senate seats and two governorships. The Communist Party is legal and active, but very small and unimportant except as an intellectual force—people in other parties still pay attention to the Communists' analyses. There are also several other smaller parties.

One of the most important events of the Betancourt years was a Venezuelan initiative that would have great repercussions worldwide. In 1960, Venezuela's energy minister, Juan Pablo Pérez Alfonso, came up with the idea of an Organization of Petroleum Exporting Countries (OPEC), to stabilize prices and reduce competition among the major producers. OPEC would allocate production, assigning a maximum to be produced by each member country, and would control prices for different grades of oil worldwide. The Arab producers saw the advantage of this arrangement, and OPEC quickly became a major force in the world market. (Besides Venezuela, Ecuador is the only other Latin American member.)

Good Times, Bad Times, and Corruption (1973–1989)

In the wake of the Arab-Israeli war of October 1973, OPEC raised prices for crude oil fourfold. Venezuela suddenly found itself with $6 billion worth of extra, unexpected income just as Carlos Andrés Pérez, of Acción Democrática, was taking office as president in February 1974.

At first, President Pérez promised to "manage abundance with the mentality of scarcity." But there was so much cash that it was impossible to resist temptations to spend it liberally.

Part of the money went into a very generous foreign-aid program, including long-term loans to Central American countries so they could pay for petroleum imports. Much more of it was put into large-scale, high-technology industrial development projects. The greatest of these was a complex of steel, aluminum, and bauxite refineries in Ciudad Guayana, near Venezuela's largest deposits of iron ore and other minerals.

Other expenses were not productive. For example, the government canceled debts worth $350 million owed to it by Venezuelan farmers. The government subsidized food prices and approved wage increases, so everyone had more spending money. It also supported the *bolívar* at a high value (guaranteeing that it could be traded in at a bank for a high price in dollars), which made imports cheap—it was in this period that people bought most of those Japanese television sets that are now in almost every home. There were also big increases in the sales of German cameras and automobiles, and of clothing and processed foods from the United States. Per-capita consumption of imported Scotch whiskey—an expensive luxury—became one of the highest in the world. According to historian James Rudolph, "the Pérez administration spent more in five years than all other governments during the previous 143 years combined."

Despite its wealth, the government also borrowed heavily from international banks. It had set up semi-autonomous state firms, which could borrow on their own, independently of central government accounting. They generally took short-term loans, despite the higher interest rates, because they would receive the money more quickly. Corruption was rampant, often in the form of unjustified cost overruns by contractors and kickbacks to government officials from contractors.

But the good times were not to last. Petroleum prices leveled off in

1976 and began to fall in 1978. Also, by that year the government's foreign debt (including the debts of all those government agencies) had reached nearly $12 billion, and interest rates were rising. Pérez's successors inherited an overgrown network of state enterprises, an unpayable foreign debt, greatly decreased revenues, and a government bureaucracy and upper middle class that had gotten used to living very expensively.

Most of the population found itself suddenly much worse off, as the *bolívar* lost value (now each *bolívar* bought less foreign money, making imports more expensive), food prices rose, and public services declined. But despite the changed conditions, some people continued to live expensively. During the administration of Jaime Lusinchi (1984–1989), it was discovered that government officials were letting associates buy dollars at a special low rate, subsidized by the government, and splitting the proceeds. The scandal implicated the president himself and was terribly demoralizing to ordinary Venezuelan citizens, who had been those making sacrifices.

In 1988, Carlos Andrés Pérez won election to a second term as president, the first time this has happened since Pérez Jiménez was overthrown in 1958. He took office in 1989. But conditions had changed greatly since his first term. The treasury was nearly empty, and there was a huge foreign debt.

Customs and Culture

In Venezuela, as shown in Chapter III, Indian and African traditions enriched the Spanish culture, creating a very complex mix. And within Venezuela, each region developed its own way of speaking and its own musical and artistic traditions.

During most of Venezuela's history, the great distances and natural barriers such as mountains and dry plains, along with political and social conflicts, kept the people from different regions so far apart that they barely understood one another. Their mutual distrust was one reason for the many civil wars.

It is only in recent times, with the development of radio and especially television, that people from the different regions have become better acquainted with one another and have shed many of their old suspicions. What survives of the regional traditions is now regarded as "folklore," quaint and interesting local peculiarities, not threatening to anybody. But it is from this body of folklore that modern Venezuelan writers, musicians, and artists are drawing to create a modern, national culture.

Folk Magic and Religion

The overwhelming majority of Venezuelans consider themselves Roman Catholics, and almost all the others are also Christians, belonging to

In a folk festival in Cumaná combining Spanish and Indian elements, the Devil and a Little Indian take a rest.   Rafael Salvatore

Protestant churches and sects. But this doesn't stop them from believing in other kinds of spirits.

The combination of Christian and non-Christian religious practices has an old history in Venezuela. According to folklorist Juan Pablo Sojo, Catholic priests in colonial days often called on black sorcerers to join them in exorcisms.

The Spaniards introduced many magical beliefs, including fear of "the evil eye." An example of beliefs with African origins is found among poor black farmers in Barlovento. There each individual has a personal saint for his or her special devotion. According to anthropologist Angelina Pollak-Eltz, these substitute for the personal gods their African ancestors had in Dahomey or Nigeria, and are worshipped the same way. The *campesinos* (small farmers) "ask their saints for favors and make promises. . . . [W]hen the patron grants what the devotee has requested these promises are usually paid up scrupulously. If not the owner of the miracle statue punishes the saint by leaving the statue outdoors."

In modern times, there are two highly organized cults that are uniquely Venezuelan in origin, although each has by now acquired international adherents. One is centered on a naked lady on a tapir, the other on a sad-eyed, mustachioed man in a blue suit.

María Lionza

A statue of María Lionza, naked and astride a tapir, greets motorists on one of the main highways into Caracas. When she is not riding her tapir, she lives in a palace deep inside a mountain, surrounded by her friends the animals and the souls of people who have been devoted to her. According to anthropologist Pollak-Eltz, "María

This altar to María Lionza, in Agua Blanca, Portuguesa State, shows the goddess herself standing next to a tapir, between the Indian chief Guaicaipuro and El Negro Felipe; other Indian spirits are represented on the lower shelf. Vladimir Sersa

Lionza has aspects of the Virgin Mary, of an indigenous [Indian] nature divinity, and of an African goddess."

Her believers are almost all Roman Catholics who also firmly believe in the Christian God, Jesus Christ, and the Virgin Mary. However, for practical results they turn to María Lionza. Her priests, called *bancos*, are believed to be able to summon spiritual powers to cure cancer and other diseases, solve love problems, and resolve economic difficulties. Cigars, candles, and sometimes a surgeon's costume are used in the rituals. All the *bancos*, who may be either men or women, ask is to be paid according to the ability of the client. Unlike Christian priests and ministers, they make no demands on their clients to reform their conduct.

The most important spirits are "The Three Powers": María Lionza herself, represented as a beautiful white woman; a black man known as El Negro Felipe, and the Indian chief Guaicaipuro—who is shown with feathers in a headband, like a Hollywood movie Indian (the real Guaicaipuro did not use such an ornament). In addition to these, the *bancos* can summon spirits from numerous "courts" made up of figures believed to be powerful. For example, the Celestial Court is made up of Catholic saints; the Court of the Indians is made up of the great Indian chiefs of Venezuela's history; an African Court includes not only seven Yoruba deities but also a spirit called the Great Viking, and a Court of Simón Bolívar also includes Hitler and Stalin. Obviously, these groupings are not logical or historical, but magical: Things are put together that the *banco* thinks have a similar kind of magic power.

This cult is now nationwide and has even spread to neighboring countries, but it seems to have originated in the Venezuelan state of Yaracuy, in the west. Historians and folklorists have come up with ingenious theories about its origins, some claiming it comes from a real landowner named María Alonso, or perhaps María de la Onza, in colonial times. Pollak-Eltz offers the simplest and most plausible explanation: Before the arrival of the Spaniards, the Indians believed that female spirits lived in and protected the hills and streams, and María Lionza—who lives in the mountain Sorte—is one of them, with a new name and the addition of many other beliefs. One reason that this particular goddess survived while the others have been forgotten may be that, in the 1920's, one of dictator Juan Vicente Gómez's mistresses was a believer and provided the cult publicity and political protection. Since the cult can absorb almost any kind of magic, people just moved their old beliefs to María Lionza's kingdom.

The Miraculous Doctor
The cult of the Miraculous Doctor is based on a real physician, Dr. José Gregorio Hernández (1864–1919). He was a very successful healer, but his cures were based on scientific medicine, not miracles. He was also a deeply religious man, according to all accounts, and so generous that he often bought medicine for his patients from his own funds.

He was run over by a car in 1919—surely one of the earliest such accidents in Venezuelan history. Years after his death, he began to perform miracles. That is, people would pray to him and be cured, they say, of such ailments as respiratory diseases, a brain tumor, or infertility. Statues and pictures of the doctor are in many homes. There is a well-developed movement to have the Catholic Church declare him a saint—a long process, still under way.

Meanwhile, the *bancos* of María Lionza have adopted José Gregorio Hernández as one more source of spiritual power, along with Guaicaipuro, Bolívar, and the Great Viking.

Some Venezuelan Folk Beliefs

The following are a few of the beliefs culled by Angelina Pollak-Eltz from the mix of European, African, and Indian superstitions of Venezuela:

To cure colds and asthma, eat a roasted mouse without salt.

For a headache, split a lemon and make the sign of the cross with one half on the forehead and with the other on the back of the neck. Then toss half the peel over the shoulder without looking, and the pain will go away. Whoever steps on the peel will get the pain. If the other half of the peel dries up rapidly, the headache was caused by witchcraft.

Brujos (healers) can increase virility and potency through the use of herbs and other rituals. They can also increase a woman's fertility or induce abortions. In Falcón, a woman may pulverize a bull's testicles and put the powder in a man's food to increase his sexual desire.

Literature

Until very recent times, writers in Venezuela could expect to reach only a tiny audience in their own countries, since most people were illiterate. Many of them felt alienated from the crude and often illiterate men who ran the country's ranches, farms, and mines and who governed as despots. Their writings, then, tended to be either formal exercises in elegance for that tiny educated elite or were angry denunciations of the barbarous customs and cruel natural forces from which they felt estranged.

At the very beginning, the country's most influential and prolific

A chapel venerating the Miraculous Doctor, José Gregorio Hernández, near Ortiz, his birthplace, in the state of Guárico. Vladimir Sersa

writer was the man chiefly responsible for its independence, Simón Bolívar. Besides his many other activities, the Liberator wrote thousands of letters, ranging from personal love notes to philosophical reflections to analyses of political and military strategy, which are graceful and eloquent and couched in the formal language of the eighteenth century. He also wrote a poem, the original Constitution of Bolivia, several major speeches, and numerous decrees. Andrés Bello (1781–1865), who had been one of Bolívar's tutors, wrote major studies of philology and law as well as poetry and critical essays. In 1829, he moved to Chile, where he became the first president of the national university. Caracas honors his memory in the Catholic University Andrés Bello.

In 1840, Antonio Leocadio Guzmán (1801–1884; the father of President Antonio Guzmán Blanco) founded a newspaper, *El Venezolano*, to print his articles promoting his new Liberal party. Other important historians and essayists were Fermín Toro (1807–1865) and Juan Vicente González (1810–1866).

Eduardo Blanco (1838–1912) wrote a work that would influence both historical writing and fiction, which have often been combined in Venezuela. *Venezuela heróica* (*Heroic Venezuela*) is a feverishly exciting account of some of the battles for independence, in which Bolívar and the other patriots seem as ferocious and exemplary as the heroes of a Greek epic. In the novel *Peonía* (the name of a sugar plantation), by Manuel Vicente Romero (1865–1917), similarly simplified, unrealistic characters struggle against the forces of nature and the injustices of society.

The Nicaraguan poet Rubén Darío (1867–1916), founder of a new lyrical style he called "Modernism," strongly influenced Venezuelan writers by his emphasis on poetic form. Important Venezuelan Modernists were the poets Rufino Blanco Fombona (1874–1944) and Alfredo Arvelo Larriva (1883–1934), and the novelist Manuel Díaz Rodríguez.

Besides poetry, Blanco Fombona wrote a biography of Bolívar (always a favorite subject for Venezuelan authors), short stories, and novels bitterly satirizing Venezuelan customs.

Venezuela's most famous novelist is Rómulo Gallegos (1884–1969), and his most famous novel is *Doña Bárbara*, published in 1929 (an English translation, with the same title, was published in 1931). Others include *Cantaclaro* (1934), about a singing *llanero* (*Cantaclaro*, literally "sings clear," is a nickname for someone who speaks his mind), and *Canaima* (1935), about a struggle against nature and human evil in the Venezuelan Guayana.

Teresa de la Parra (the pen name of Ana Teresa Parra Sanojo, 1890–1936) is Venezuela's most celebrated woman novelist—so far— and the first novelist to treat the inner, psychological life of women in Venezuela. *Mama Blanca's Souvenirs*, one of the small number of her works translated into English, deals with a girl's life on a plantation.

The "Generation of 1918," made up of poets a little younger than Gallegos and de la Parra, rebelled against Modernism, stressing content rather than form. Andrés Eloy Blanco (1897–1955), who was imprisoned by Gómez, is the best known of the group.

The 1928 revolt against the Gómez dictatorship produced not only many of the country's future political leaders but also some of its most important writers. Arturo Uslar Pietri (1906–   ), who in his long career has written novels, short stories, plays, and many books of essays, is one of the most important. His most famous novel, *Red Lances* (first published in 1931; translated in 1963), deals with ironies of Venezuela's independence wars, when Venezuelan slaves fought against the patriots.

Miguel Otero Silva (1908–1985), also from the Generation of 1928, was a poet, journalist and novelist whose harsh criticisms of Venezuelan social conditions are sometimes relieved with a dose of humor. The

The Many Lives of
Doña Bárbara

Rómulo Gallegos's *Doña Bárbara* is the most widely read novel ever produced in Venezuela, and the subject of many films and dramas. It has also played a role in the country's politics.

Doña is an old-fashioned title of respect for a woman (equivalent to *don* for men), and Doña Bárbara, as her name suggests, is a woman who is powerful and barbaric. She controls a vast ranch in the Llanos, and through murder, bribery, and intimidation—aided by black magic—subjects men to her will. She is opposed by Santos Luzardo, a younger and more educated man, newly arrived from the city, who refuses to give in to her as he struggles to reclaim property that is rightfully his.

The novel's most obvious literary ancestor is *Facundo: Civilization and Barbarism*, in which the Argentine writer and politician Domingo Faustino Sarmiento used a real historical character, Facundo Quiroga, the way Gallegos uses Doña Bárbara, to represent the primitive violence of the countryside. Sarmiento's book started him off on a literary and political career that eventually, in 1868, made him president of Argentina. Gallegos's novel did the same for him. Gallegos's characters are less complex than Sarmiento's, however—Facundo at least has some brief inner conflicts. But Doña

subject matter of his novels ranges over opposition to Gómez (*Fiebre* [*Fever*]; 1928), life in the oil fields (*Oficina No. 1* [*Office No. 1*]; 1961), the decline of rural towns (*Casas muertas* [*Dead Houses*]; 1955), prob-

Bárbara and Santos Luzardo are powerful symbols of two social forces—rural "barbarism" versus urban "civilization."

The book appeared in 1929, just a year after the revolt that shook the dictatorship of Juan Vicente Gómez. Gómez believed—probably correctly—that the tyranny of Doña Bárbara was a disguised portrait of his own regime, and Gallegos had to go into exile. Naturally, the novel became extremely popular among the dictator's many opponents. In 1943, a film version, for which Gallegos wrote the script, was made in Mexico and was very successful internationally.

When Gallegos returned to Venezuela after Gómez's death, he became active in politics, and in 1947, he was elected president—in large part owing to his fame as the author of *Doña Bárbara*.

In 1974, when a television version (in thirty-four segments) was made in Venezuela, screenwriter José Ignacio Cabrujas was surprised to find that even his maid had read the book—it was, she said, the only book she had ever read, and she loved it. But she had given it a feminist interpretation—in her view, Doña Bárbara was the heroine, rightfully trying to protect her property and her independence from the city slicker, Santos Luzardo. Cabrujas took this interpretation into account, making the ranchwoman more sympathetic than he might have otherwise.

There have been other dramatizations of *Doña Bárbara*, and at this writing a new television series, to be jointly produced with Mexico, is in the works.

lems of youth in Caracas in the 1970's (*Cuando quiero llorar no lloro* [*When I Want to Cry I Can't*]—a line from a poem by Rubén Darío)— and the sixteenth-century rampage of Lope de Aguirre *(Aguirre)*. Ramón

Díaz Sánchez introduced the theme of conflicts in the oil fields with his novel *Mene* (the name of a fictional town; 1936).

Guillermo Meneses (1911–1978) was another journalist, novelist, and short-story writer. His novel *Campeones* (*Champions;* 1939) has been made into a television series, but he is even better known for his intricately crafted short stories, with supernatural overtones reminiscent of Edgar Allan Poe.

The abuses of Pérez Jiménez's regime are the subject of José Vicente Abreu's excruciating novel *Se llamaba S.N.* (*Its Name Was S.N.*, Seguridad Nacional—the secret police; 1985). In recent years, several novels have dealt with Venezuela's *guerrilla* war of the 1960's, mostly from the point of view of the *guerrillas*. These include Luis Correa's *FALN—Brigada Uno* (*FALN—Brigade One*, which was the "brigade" assigned to Caracas; 1973), Adriano González Leon's *País portátil* (*Portable Country;* 1968), and probably the best and certainly the most complex of the lot, *Abrapalabra* (literally, *Open, Word!*, a play on "abracadabra"; 1979), by Luis Britto García. José Balza also refers to the *guerrilla* war in *Setecientas palmeras plantadas en el mismo lugar* (*Seven Hundred Palm Trees Planted in the Same Place;* 1974), although the book is primarily an experiment in different ways to tell the same story. Balza is also an important literary critic.

Eduardo Liendo (1941–   ), an FALN *guerrilla*, was captured, exiled, and finally pardoned—but his most popular book is a hilarious, surrealist comedy on an entirely different theme, one that has become very important in contemporary Venezuela. *El mago de la cara de vidrio* (*The Glass-Faced Magician;* 1973) is about a television set that takes over a family, telling the members what to buy and how to behave—as told by the TV set's opponent, the head of the family, driven to an insane asylum after attacking the set with a baseball bat.

The Impact of Television

The "glass-faced magician," television, is more highly developed in Venezuela than in any other country in Latin America, and it has transformed the country in many ways. But attacking it with a baseball bat may not be a good idea, because not all of its magic has been evil.

Marketing statistics show that more than 90 percent of Venezuelan households have television—and many houses have several sets. In Caracas, almost 98 percent of the households have at least one TV. This is an amazingly high figure, much higher than for any other country in Latin America. In comparison, only 39 percent of the households have a telephone. Even the most wretched shacks on the hillsides of Caracas have television antennas. Moreover, most of these sets are on for several hours a day.

The "glass-faced magician" on the road in Puerto La Cruz, Anzoátegui State. Rafael Salvatore

There are two main explanations for the spread of the power of this "magician." First, the sudden and unexpected wealth from petroleum, especially in the mid-1970's after OPEC raised its prices, raised the value of the Venezuelan currency and made it very cheap to import goods—and one of the biggest imports was television sets, along with video cassette recorders and other electronic products. Second, Venezuelan TV stations were producing programs that people wanted to watch.

Television in many countries is very dull. Local production facilities are usually poor, and the station managers fill the time with old movies. Government censorship may keep any challenging ideas off the air, and a lack of competition slows down any impulse to try something new.

Not in Venezuela. Here there are two powerful television stations locked in intense competition for Venezuela's huge audience: Radio Caracas Televisión and Venevisión. They try to "steal" one another's writers, actors, and musicians, by offering them more pay, and each tries to catch the other off guard by coming up with surprising twists in programming—a more daring news investigation, a funnier comedy, a more violent or sexier dramatic serial, and so on.

And that's not all. The other stations, including Channel 8, run by the government, have also thought up plans which allow them to retain their segment of the national audience. The result of all this competition is not always thoughtful programming, but it almost always is exciting.

Production qualities are very high, because the stations can afford investments in the latest equipment and in expert personnel. Because of the huge audience, advertisers pay well, and the stations also make

This is one of several popular magazines devoted to telenovelas *and other television programming in Venezuela. Top billing here is given to Robert Avellanet, a fourteen-year old Puerto Rican in the well-known group Menudo. "El Puma," Venezuelan singer José Luis Rodríguez, is said to have filled Madison Square Garden. Jeannette Rodríguez is a Venezuelan actress who has starred in many* telenovelas.

TELE
NOVELAS
...Y TODO EN TELEVISION

AÑO I - Nº 32

LOS MEJORES CHISMES DE TIA CLEOTILDE

ROBERT SE CONFIESA:

¡LAS VENTAJAS Y DESVENTAJAS DE menudo !

BLOQUE EDITORIAL
DE ARMAS

EL PUMA LLENO EL MADISON

PRECIO
EN VENEZUELA
Bs. 30,00
EN EL EXTERIOR
US$ 2.00

JEANNETTE
¡SUSPENDIDAS LAS GRABACIONES DE ''POBRE DIABLA''!

"Poor Family 1" by Marisol, Venezuela's leading sculptress. Courtesy Marisol/
VAGA, New York 1991

money by exporting their programs. Venezuelan *telenovelas* (television
novels)—dramatic serials that may go on for a hundred or more epi-
sodes—are popular throughout Latin America, and are even shown in
Spain, Italy, China, and many other countries. Americans living in areas
reached by one of the two Spanish-language networks in the United
States (Telemundo and Univision) can almost certainly tune into a
Venezuelan *telenovela* every night.

*A hanging sculpture by Venezuelan artist Jesús Soto, a leading member of the kinetic art
movement that gained international prominence in the 1970's.* Vladimir Sersa

This is an impressive fact, because it means that Venezuela is successfully competing for an international audience against such major exporters of dramatic serials as Brazil, Mexico, and Argentina—all of which have much larger populations and more highly developed movie industries. (There is hardly any moviemaking in Venezuela—screenwriters, directors, and actors all go into television instead.)

Television's impact on other areas of culture has been very great. For one thing, it has made it possible for musicians and other creative artists from formerly isolated little towns to reach a national audience. It has also made the artists themselves more aware of one another's work, so that it is easier to borrow techniques and create new ways of expressing old traditions. There is even a group from San Fernando de Apure that uses a saxophone instead of the traditional harp, playing traditional music of the Llanos in jazz arrangements.

Another result has been that the regional differences have become much less important. People from all over the country are now beginning to speak more or less the same way, or at least to understand the unusual words from distant regions. There is also more of a sense that they are all fellow Venezuelans, and when disaster strikes—such as a flood that occurred a few years ago—people from throughout the country respond to the televised news by sending donations.

Today, "high" culture—the works produced by and for the educated minority—and popular or "folk" culture are all part of Venezuelan art, with many mutual borrowings from both sides. This is why *telenovelas* and literary fiction need to be understood together; there is scarcely a novel written in Venezuela today that does not refer explicitly to the widespread viewing of television, and there is scarcely a *telenovela* that hasn't felt the touch of some major and quite respectable Venezuelan intellectual.

Daily Life

Venezuela is a highly urbanized society, where everyone is exposed not only to television but to all the mass media and where, except for the Caracas subway, everyone and everything depends on automotive transport. So it is not surprising that some of the problems most complained about are traffic jams and information overload. Today 88 percent of the people of Venezuela live in towns of 20,000 inhabitants or more, and nearly a third live in the four largest cities: Caracas, Maracaibo, Valencia, and Barquisimeto.

The problems of these cities have become more serious in the past ten years, as Venezuelans have seen the purchasing power of their earnings shrink and as the national and local governments have been strapped for funds. Daily life today reflects the adaptations people have had to make to the changed circumstances.

Education

To cope with all the information, Venezuelans have one of the most extensive school systems in the Americas. Almost all the young people in Venezuela, and many who are not so young, go to school. Education is compulsory through the eighth grade, but the constitution guarantees access to free public education at all levels, from preschool through university. There are now more than 6 million students, almost one out of every three Venezuelans.

Although President Antonio Guzmán Blanco introduced compulsory, universal education back in 1870, the major growth in the school system has occurred in the past thirty years. According to the 1981 census, nearly 60 percent of people over 65 had had no schooling at all, whereas only 7.6 percent of youth aged 15 to 19 had had no schooling. Only 15.3 percent of the population over 15 years of age was illiterate (one of the lowest rates in Latin America), and most of these are 45 years of age or older.

The system is highly centralized. A child in the Andes uses the same books as a child in the same grade in the Orinoco Delta, or in the Llanos, or in Caracas. In contrast to the United States, where state and local governments raise most of the money for public schools, in Venezuela the central government pays almost all the costs (96 percent) for education. The 1989 budget allotted $1 billion to education, one fifth of the total national budget.

However, this money is not necessarily spent where it is most needed. A disproportionate share goes to higher education, while many of the public primary schools are so overcrowded they are holding two or even three sessions a day.

Although private-school students are only about 13 percent of the total student population in the country, graduates from private schools

The High Cost of College

Unlike most countries, Venezuela spends more per student in higher education (colleges and universities) than in primary schools and preschool. Although higher education has only 8 percent of the students, it receives 29 percent of the education budget.

Free tuition has made it easy for some people to become professional students, hanging on as undergraduates until they are well into their thirties. Congress has been considering a law that would permit schools to charge tuition in some cases—for example, when students keep failing and repeating the same courses, or when they finish one undergraduate degree and then start on another one.

make up a disproportionately large percentage of students in public universities—47 percent of those at the Universidad Central de Venezuela, or UCV (Central University), and 78 percent at Simón Bolívar University. Private institutions of higher learning account for only 18 percent of university students.

Venezuela has seventeen universities and forty-seven other institutions of higher learning (including junior colleges, teachers' colleges, and technical institutes). The oldest is the Central University, founded in 1721.

Sports

When they're not studying, Venezuelans are likely to be at a baseball game, either playing or watching. Baseball is a national passion.

A cockfight in El Calvario, a neighborhood of Caracas.
Vladimir Sersa

Professional teams from Caracas, La Guaira, Magallanes, Aragua, Lara, and Zulia compete in a four-month season, and the winner goes to the Caribbean Series, to play against the champions of Puerto Rico, Mexico, and the Dominican Republic. Among the Venezuelans who have played in the major leagues in recent years have been the home-run hitter Antonio (Tony) Armas, catcher Baudilio Díaz, outfielder Manny Trillo, and pitchers Luis Leal, Manuel Sarmiento, Luis Aponte, and Luis M. Sánchez. Over 200,000 children between the ages of five and eighteen participate in the Little League organization *Los Criollitos*, and there are also many amateur adult teams throughout the country.

Soccer is also important, especially in the Andean region, with the best teams in Mérida, Portuguesa, Lara, and Táchira—although every major city has a team. In basketball, the most famous team is the Guaiqueríes from the island of Margarita. Track and field are also popular, as is boxing. In amateur boxing, Morochito Rodríguez won an Olympic gold medal. Venezuelan professional world boxing champions have included Morocho Hernández, Lumumba Estaba, Betulio González, Antonio Gómez, Alfredo Marcano, Vicente Paúl Rondón, and Rafael Oronó.

Horse-racing has probably been going on since the *conquistadores* brought the first horses over from Spain. Today there are racetracks in

"Toros coleados"—trying to tumble a bull by pulling its tail—on the patron saint's feast day in Elorza, state of Apure. Vladimir Sersa

at least six cities, the most important being La Rinconada in Caracas, which has ponds, parks, restaurants, stalls for fifteen hundred thoroughbreds, electronic scoreboards, lights, and so on. Every week bettors at off-track betting offices place millions of dollars on the horses

· 153 ·

in a system called "five and six"—to win, a bettor has to pick the winning horse in each of five or, for the biggest prizes, of six races.

Other games brought over from Spain include bullfighting and cockfighting. Cockfighting is not precisely a sport, since only the birds compete, but it is followed passionately by many Venezuelans. There are cockpits in almost every little town and many neighborhoods of the bigger towns. Bullfighting arenas are much more elegant and, of course, much larger. The city of Valencia claims to have the biggest bullfighting arena in the world.

There is also a very dangerous variation on bullfighting called *toros coleados*, or "tailing the bull," which seems to have been invented in Venezuela. It was already common in the Llanos before independence. A bull is let loose with a whack to get it running, and a player on horseback chases after it and tries to grab its tail and pull it off its feet. Often it's the bull that pulls the rider down, and many *coleadores* have broken their heads or hands in their falls. Although the horsemen these days wear helmets, the sport is still extremely hazardous.

Night Life

A favorite activity of Venezuelans, from colonial times to the present, has always been dancing. Simón Bolívar was a tireless dancer of mazurkas and contradanzas. Styles have changed, of course. And in the past ten years, with the shrinking of people's purchasing power, tensions between the rich and poor have increased, and so have the differences in their style of partying.

The *discotecas* (discotheques) that were popular in the 1970's have mostly disappeared. Instead, in the poorer neighborhoods, a group of young people will simply gather at a streetcorner or a bus stop with a few bottles of Venezuelan rum and a cassette player. These Friday- and Saturday-night outdoor parties are noisy and sometimes turn violent as the kids get drunk and wild, causing more tensions between the classes, but there's no place else for them to go.

Wealthier young people, especially those in the eastern affluent neighborhoods of Caracas, now have private clubs just outside the city limits—another new development. Students at the Central University, which has a subculture all its own, hold *verbenas*, parties where they sell food and drinks to raise money for their university department or club.

For young people who are neither rich nor poor, invitations to parties now are likely to say *"traje"* (a pun on *traje*, suit, and the past tense of *traer*, to bring). This means "Bring Your Own" refreshments. This is another way people have adapted to the economic situation—a few years ago, a host would have been offended if a guest brought his or her own liquor.

What a visitor is likely to hear at any of these parties these days is *Tecno Pop*—African-American–style rap but with lyrics in Spanish. The tapes are usually by Latin Americans in the United States—one popular specialist in *"rapear"* is the Venezuelan Jorge Fonseca, who lives in the United States. To *Tecno Pop*, party-goers do their own version of break dancing. Also popular is a fusion of *salsa* and rap, equally fast-paced with short, rhymed verses. For a change of pace, someone may put on some slow-tempo, romantic ballads, perhaps sung by Ricardo Montaner, Franco de Vita, or Yordano, three popular Venezuelan performers.

Another of the favorite activities is going to see an American movie. In 1987, Venezuela imported 807 feature-length films, 74 percent of them from the United States. This is almost twice as many as Colombia, and four times as many as Brazil, which has eight times as many people as Venezuela. There is a great fondness for U.S. films, music, and clothes. To most Venezuelans today, the United States is the model of a more technically advanced and wealthier civilization, just as Paris was in the days of Guzmán Blanco.

The Caracas Metro

Some things in Caracas work very well. One of those is the Caracas Metro, or subway, which the *caraqueños* treat with loving care.

Many years in construction—so many that people had despaired of its ever getting completed—the Metro finally opened in 1983, and its lines have been extended since then. It now runs from the extreme east to the extreme west and the southwest of the metropolitan area, rapidly, quietly and cheaply—fares run to about the equivalent of ten U.S. cents. Each station, and in a sense the system as a whole, is conceived as a work of art—literally, because each station has a major work of sculpture at the entrance or artwork inside. These are modern, colorful, imaginative pieces by such designers as Carlos Raúl Villanueva, best known as the architect of the campus of the Central University of Venezuela.

But there is something else, besides the efficiency and beauty of the system, that is extremely impressive. That is the behavior of the thousands and thousands of people who ride the trains every day. Whereas above ground, city life seems chaotic, noisy, and rude, downstairs all is quiet and courteous. People do not smoke on the trains as they do almost anywhere else, they do not shout insults as they do when they are caught in street traffic, they do not even appear angry when they have to stand in line to buy tickets.

Caraqueños themselves are amazed at how courteous they can be to one another. They explain it as the result of a very effective public education campaign before the subway opened, stressing that "It's your system, to serve you, and you—the citizen—must take care of it." And they do.

The Caracas Metro, which is a subway for most of its length, passes aboveground through the eastern barrios. Vladimir Sersa

Life in Caracas

Metropolitan Caracas, with about 3.3 million people, is a bustling city with many attractive features. Not only is the climate delightful, the city has the good fortune to be in a valley that runs east and west, the same direction that the winds blow—they keep the air clean, sweeping away the automobile exhaust fumes and other pollution from most of the city.

In Sabana Grande there are row after row of outdoor cafés, comfortable places for a cheap date or a gathering. Groups of intellectuals meet at El Gran Café or one of its competitors at a certain time, and never need a clubhouse. Around the Plaza Bolívar in the oldest section of town, where the government palace is, tucked into the old buildings are shops and restaurants for all kinds of budgets. And the Teresa Carreño Theater, with its several performance areas and extensive backstage facilities, is said to be the finest modern theater in Latin America.

Despite an impressive complex of superhighways, one of the major annoyances of life in the city is the terrible traffic jams. The main cause

Francisco Narváez's sculpture Las Toninas (The Porpoises) *graces an area of middle-class apartments in the eastern Caracas district of El Silencio. In the background are the twin towers of the Centro Simón Bolívar, housing government offices.* Vladimir Sersa

has been the sudden, unplanned growth of the city. In just thirty-five years, beginning with the massive construction projects of Marcos Pérez Jiménez and continuing in spurts every time a rise in oil prices made money available, Caracas was transformed from a quiet little "town of red tiled roofs," centered on the old colonial city, to a modern metropolis. High-rise office buildings and shopping centers have sprung up in the middle of what used to be residential or small-scale manufacturing districts, without any regard for the additional traffic they would cause.

The *Barrios*

"*Barrio*" simply means neighborhood, but in Venezuela it implies a special kind of poor neighborhood, where people have taken over empty land and built their shacks, or "*ranchos*." *Ranchos* of cardboard, flattened metal cans, packing-crate boards, and canvas cling to the slopes and fill the gullies around all of Venezuela's major cities. A 1990 survey found 3,796 *barrios* in Venezuela, up from 2,675 only six years earlier. In metropolitan Caracas, it seems likely that about a third of the 3.3 million people live in the *barrios*.

People create a *barrio* by moving onto vacant land, usually in an organized group. Whether the land is publicly or privately owned, governments since 1958 have generally let people stay once they have their simple houses up. It has been the cheapest solution to the housing crisis.

Although they usually have no water lines, sewage system, or electricity at the beginning, the invaders do have one great advantage over most other city residents: They don't pay rent. Most of them put the money that otherwise would go to rent into improving their homes, and after a few years the cardboard and canvas *ranchos* turn into brick houses, sometimes with two or three stories. The latecomers, who arrived after the vacant land had all been taken, do have to pay rent, however—

which is why they look for new land to take over, and the number of *barrios* is increasing.

By now, the older *barrios* have paved streets and paths, and most of them have water lines, sewers, and electric lines—often strung up illegally, by tapping into a nearby utility pole. Some of these *barrios* have hundreds of thousands of inhabitants.

In some of the older *barrios*, the original settlers tried to reserve spaces for schools, playgrounds, and other open spaces. But these areas have not always been respected by later arrivals, and other *barrios* have grown without any such regulation. Most have almost no public space, for either children or adults.

Children play on the paths that wind around the houses, on the steep cement stairways, and in the streets. The smaller boys play *chapita*, a poor boy's version of baseball—they toss up bottlecaps and try to hit them with a broomstick. Some of them play handball, if they can find the space and a wall. Young girls make houses and dolls out of cans, and play "mommy and daddy" with their littler brothers and sisters.

The people in the *barrios* have been the most seriously affected by the economic decline of the past ten years. Many have lost their jobs, and those who are still working can't make ends meet on their wages. Crime has also increased in these past ten years, and those winding pathways and steep stairways now can be very dangerous. Young criminals, called "*malandros*," charge housewives a "toll" for going up and down stairs, and there are frequent reports of assaults and even murders for small amounts of money. In many cases the motive is drugs.

Running a Small Business in a *Barrio*

At the eastern end of Caracas, a cement-paved street leaves the highway to wind through the *barrio* José Félix Rivas—named for a hero of the independence wars. The sweet, heavy odor of traffic fumes gives way

Bloques *(high-rise apartment buildings) in the 23 de Enero (January 23rd) housing project, originally built by Marcos Pérez Jiménez for army officers, are now occupied by low-income civilian families and surrounded by a typical* barrio *of houses built by other low-income families.*   Vladimir Sersa

to smells of frying cornmeal and the iron taste of the fine red dust. On the slopes on either side, redbrick houses, some two and three stories high, crowd so tightly they seem to climb on top of one another.

Although it is only five P.M. and the street is full of people talking, lounging, or coming home from work, most of the shops are shut tight with *santamarías*—steel security curtains that have been closed permanently since the riots that tore through the community in 1989 (see Chapter X). But here and there a few stores are open for business— some with assistance from a private Venezuelan charitable organization, the Eugenio Mendoza Foundation.

Juan Paredes, a robust, bluff-talking man in his mid-thirties, owns a hardware store he calls "Zone 6." His rented space is about twelve feet wide and twice as deep, crammed with building supplies, tools, paints, and a bulky punch press.

Before he took the foundation's course in basic accounting and management, he says, his accounting system was simple. He scribbled down what he was owed and what he had spent and then tried to remember which pocket held which scraps of paper.

Now he has more "control" and knows what his net earnings are: 10,000 to 12,000 bolívars ($238–285) a month. He has taken out a loan through the foundation for the equivalent of $700, and used part of it to buy a photocopying machine, an additional service for his clients. His biggest problem is the general atmosphere of lawlessness, from petty theft to massive violence.

In the 1989 riots, there was heavy destruction in José Félix Rivas and several deaths from police and army shootings. Since then, says Paredes, police have stayed out of the neighborhood, and assaults on stores are constant. The butcher shop next door had been robbed three or four times a day for the past six months, he says.

How does he cope? "Well, asking God for help. Nothing else. And getting along with them," the bad guys—up to a point.

" 'Give me a bolívar, give me a cigarette, give me some coffee, hey, let me have a screw or a bolt.' It's a tax. But then suddenly you blow up. 'What the hell is this, huh? Every day?' So then three, four days go by, and then they're back again."

Paredes suddenly shouts out to a man passing by.

"*Caballero!* You going to pay your debt one of these days?"

The man answers with a comic grimace and the promise of "Tuesday." Parades answers, "All right. Tuesday we'll talk."

Paredes' policy seems to work. During the riots, his was one of the few businesses saved, by the same young men who were trashing others.

A small entrepreneur at work in his shoemaker's shop in Plan de Manzano, a barrio *of Caracas. Signs say "No work accepted without payment," "Shoes will be thrown out or sold after 30 days," and "Welding done at your home."* Vladimir Sersa

"No, not here," they'd shout. A community center just a few doors from him was completely destroyed.

Nearby, Nestor Gamarra saved his little variety store by "infiltrating" the mobs, as he put it. He and his relatives would mingle and shout, "No, not here, let's go over to ———," naming some other neighborhood.

Across the street, a young widow, Ginelda Ascaglia, has an even smaller variety store, raised several feet above the street, accessible by high concrete steps. Her stock—shaving cream and toothpaste, batteries, and other odds and ends—is so small that she brings it back from the wholesaler once a week in shopping bags, on the subway. Perhaps because it was so small, her store did not suffer in the riots.

"I'm surviving, but I don't have money in the bank," she says. When she works "complete"—long hours, every day—she can make about $348 a month for herself and her fifteen-year-old son. Usually she makes less.

These monthly net incomes, $238–348, are barely enough to lift the entrepreneurs' families out of "extreme" poverty and into the category of "moderate" poverty, as defined by government planning agencies. This means they can afford the minimum necessities but no more, which makes them slightly better off than most of their neighbors.

In the 1960's and 1970's, institutions like the Mendoza Foundation were advocating an entirely different approach for the *barrios*, known as "community development." Community workers tried to help local residents create democratic institutions, called *juntas*, that would work for improvements of the entire *barrio*. Projects often included building stairways or paving a street, with the volunteer labor of people in the community. But in the mid-1970's, oil money and the lavish government expenditures made grass-roots organizations seem pointless—for residents it was quicker and easier to demand that the government pave a street than to do it themselves. Lately, especially since the riots, there have been signs of a return to collective community action through "neighbors' associations," to demand services and settle local disputes, but these are still in their infancy.

The philosophy of the micro-entrepreneur program is precisely the opposite, emphasizing private accumulation in the hope that enough prosperous individuals can improve the character of the community. It will, however, require much larger changes in the national economy, including an increase in the spending power of their customers, before these businesses can produce any noticeable effect in the *barrios*.

Venezuela Today: Challenges and Hopes

Overview

The most obvious problems facing Venezuela today are results of the sudden economic decline after years of rapid expansion. The country must find ways to pay a $35-billion foreign debt without further impoverishing its people. It must also cope with and try to reverse the deterioration of urban services and to halt the widening of the gap between rich and poor, which may have dangerous consequences.

But besides the economic problems, which are first on the minds of people in the government, Venezuela must also deal with a serious political challenge.

After over thirty years of stable, democratically elected governments, the Venezuelan system seems to be stuck. The government remains so highly centralized that it is not responsive to local demands. Although

Caracas, viewed from Mount Avila.   Margot Hernández

the president and other national officials are elected, many of the most powerful people in government, such as the heads of ministries and various state agencies, are not, and they have often given the impression of not caring what ordinary citizens think of what they are doing. And even high elected officials have recently been caught in flagrant abuses of power, using their positions to enrich themselves while the country they were supposed to be taking care of became poorer.

These abuses and the unresponsiveness have led to a general cynicism about the law and the authorities which no doubt contribute to the rise in crime. Cynicism also keeps people from getting actively involved

Barrio *Los lanos in San Bernardino, Caracas.*   Margot Hernández

in efforts to find new solutions to the economic and social problems. For these reasons, recent efforts to reinvigorate Venezuelan democracy and to bring corrupt government officials to trial may in the long run be as important as Venezuela's negotiations with the International Monetary Fund and the World Bank over the terms of repayment of the debt.

The nationwide rioting of 1989, which broke out just weeks after President Carlos Andrés Pérez had been inaugurated in an extravagant and highly publicized ceremony, sharply illustrated the dangers of ignoring these problems. It caught the government completely by surprise.

The Riots of February and March 1989

The violence of "Black Monday," February 27, 1989, began at the bus stops at about six in the morning in Guarenas, a working-class suburb a few miles east of Caracas. The IMF conditions its loans on economic reforms in the borrowing countries. A condition for further loans to Venezuela was that the government raise the price of gasoline that it sells to Venezuelan consumers, which is currently the lowest in the world. The IMF's reasoning was that this higher price would give the Venezuelan government more income for paying back its debts. However, a rise in the price of gasoline causes all other prices to rise as well (because almost all goods are transported by gasoline-fueled cars and trucks), making life much harder on people whose incomes stay the same.

The previous Friday, the newly elected government, bowing to pressure from the International Monetary Fund (IMF), had announced gasoline and transportation price increases. That was bad enough, but when people tried to go to work, they found that the bus owners had raised fares even more. Already fed up with shortages of corn flour, milk, and other necessities, they blew up, first destroying the buses, then going after the supermarkets.

Consumers were angry at the shopkeepers because they had been holding back goods, causing the shortages. The shopkeepers were not entirely to blame, however—the economy was so unstable that they were sure prices were about to rise, which meant that anything they sold at the lower price today they would have trouble replacing at higher prices tomorrow.

A special edition of the newsmagazine Momento, *commemorating the first anniversary of the riots that broke out on February 27, 1989, says "A Thousand Deaths and Nothing Changes." The actual number of deaths is unknown.*

· 168 ·

MOMENTO

EDICION ESPECIAL

A Un Año del 27 de Febrero

MIL MUERTOS Y NADA CAMBIO

PRECIO EN VENEZUELA
Bs. 35,00
EN EL EXTERIOR
US$ 1.50

BLOQUE EDITORIAL DEARMAS

Stimulated by radio and television reports of what was going on in Guarenas, other commuters began rioting at the main Caracas bus terminal, and by early afternoon the riots had spread across the country.

"It was an explosion," according to a priest with long experience in the *barrios*. "It was an overflowing, with no control and in my judgment no leadership." To the middle class, it seemed that the "hills"—the *barrios*—were descending on the city. "They came down like ants," says the priest.

Intensive television coverage of the first hours of rioting contributed to its rapid spread. Viewers saw crowds breaking into stores and the police, perplexed and unprepared, letting it happen. In some cases, the police tried to bring order to the pillage, telling people to take food but not to damage the stores, or letting groups into the stores ten at a time. By the time the news coverage was pulled from the air, the rioting had spread to Valencia, Zulia, and other regions.

The next day was much worse. Worker absenteeism was reported to be 98 percent; doctors, police, and journalists were almost the only ones at work. Professional thieves and amateurs, taking advantage of the general confusion, broke into other stores, stealing television sets, VCRs, furniture, even notebooks and pencils. In the frenzy, groups of youths tore heavy mechanical chairs out of barbershops and either abandoned them in the street or threw them over precipices.

The government decreed an eight-P.M.-to-dawn curfew, announced a temporary suspension of certain constitutional rights, and called in the army, landing planeloads of heavily armed troops at the Caracas airport, La Carlota. The army, untrained in police work, behaved as though operating against a foreign enemy.

According to the report by Amnesty International, the army and police seized and even shot innocent people who were in the riot zones. Armor-piercing bullets punched through *rancho* walls and killed people sitting peacefully at home. These actions further enraged people in the *barrios* and led to further destruction. In some areas, even schools and community centers with no connection to the government were torn apart.

The official army count was 277 dead, but most observers believe there were many more. In their rage, the people had destroyed the whole supply system in their neighborhoods. Also destroyed was any faith they may have had in the impartiality of the army and police.

Foreign Relations

During Carlos Andrés Pérez's first term as president (1974–1979), he took a vigorously independent position in foreign policy, coming into conflict with the United States government on several issues. First, he was critical of the involvement of the United States in the overthrow of the democratically elected government of Chile, which had just occurred in September 1973. He also established very cordial relationships with Cuba and Nicaragua, supplying arms to the Sandinistas at the same time that the United States was supplying arms to their enemies.

He saw himself as a leader forging an integration of the countries of Latin America, independent of the United States, in a modern version of Simón Bolívar's dream. He used some of Venezuela's new wealth from the 1973 rise in oil prices to promote economic cooperation and development among Latin American countries. Together with President Luis Echeverría of Mexico—another country that had benefited from the rise in oil prices—he founded the Sistema Económico Latinoamericano, or SELA (Latin American Economic System) with headquarters in Caracas, for this purpose.

The two presidents who followed, Luis Herrera Campins (1979–1984) and Jaime Lusinchi (1984–1989), were much less interested in

foreign affairs. When Carlos Andrés Pérez returned to the presidency in 1989 for a second term, he did not find a huge surplus of money but an empty treasury and a huge debt, greatly limiting his foreign-policy initiatives.

Pérez's desire for Latin American leadership probably has not changed, although he is now forced to give most of his attention to negotiations with the International Monetary Fund, which will determine the terms on which Venezuela can borrow the money it needs to pay old debts and stimulate its economy. Nevertheless, he has taken independent stands on certain issues that are very dear to his heart. He condemned the United States' invasion of Panama and has refused to recognize the new government of Guillermo Endara—not because he supported General Manuel Antonio Noriega, who was overthrown and captured, but because he protested the use of force and the continuing occupation of Panama by U.S. troops. He continues to be a confidant of Fidel Castro of Cuba, and he has played an important role in mediating conflicts between the current president of Nicaragua, Violeta Chamorro, and former president and Sandinista Party head Daniel Ortega. Venezuelan troops were a major contingent of the United Nations' peacekeeping force sent to Nicaragua to disarm the Contras (the anti-Sandinista resistance), and another Venezuelan military unit has been sent by Pérez to serve as President Chamorro's bodyguards.

Toward a Broader, Deeper Democracy

In December 1989, in response to demands from many pressure groups, Venezuelans were finally permitted to vote directly for governors, mayors, and regional officials. Up until then, political parties had run whole

An oil tanker passes under the Rafael Urdaneta Bridge, spanning 28,467 feet (8,679 meters) across petroleum-rich Lake Maracaibo. Graziano Gasparini

slates, or lists, of candidates for regional offices, and voters would pick one slate or another—not the individual candidate. And, since the beginning of the republic, state governors had always been appointed by the president.

The results shook the ruling party, Acción Democrática. Although a year earlier its candidate, Carlos Andrés Pérez, won a second term in the presidency (the first time since 1958 that an ex-president has returned to office), the party lost the governorships of nine of Venezuela's twenty states and the mayoral races in many cities. Among the states lost were the economically important ones of Zulia, Carabobo, Aragua, and Bolívar—which elected a steelworker from a small leftist party called Causa R. The state of Anzoátegui elected a socialist.

Traditional Venezuela lives on: This is a house made of bahareque *(wattle-and-daub) in Altagracia de Carora, in Lara State.*   Vladimir Sersa

According to Caracas-based journalist Joe Mann, the voters "were showing their lack of faith in AD promises and the negative impact of widespread corruption during the last AD government, headed by Dr. Jaime Lusinchi from 1984–1989."

This is probably true, and marks the first time corruption—present in Venezuela throughout its history—has become a major political issue, with an impact at the polls.

But voters also seemed to be showing their lack of faith in the entire political process. More than half of them abstained from voting, in a country where voting is legally obligatory and well over 80 percent normally vote in any national election.

AD backers had trouble accepting their defeats. In Carabobo, the National Guard was called out to put down riots, and in the other states where opposition candidates won, government bureaucrats appointed by AD have been reluctant to cooperate with the new governors. In any case, the new governors' powers are limited. They do not have independent budgets, raised by their state legislatures, as do governors in the United States and many other countries, but must depend on allotments from the central government—which is, of course, controlled by Acción Democrática.

These may just be growing pains. Leading politicians in Venezuela seem at least to have realized that decentralization of power is necessary for making the system more democratic. The task now is to make the decentralization effective by giving real power to local and state-level elected officials, and to listen to what the people have to say before another explosion like that of 1989.

Bibliography

Chapter I

Bauman, Janice, and Leni Young. *Guide to Venezuela*. Caracas: Ernesto Armitano, editor, 1987. 925 pp. This is easily the most thorough and reliable guide available to all of Venezuela. Besides the usual and necessary tourist information, it is packed with historical discussions and anecdotes.

Chapter II

Botting, Douglas. *Humboldt and the Cosmos*. New York: Harper & Row, 1973. 295 pp. More than a biography, this is a beautifully illustrated and engagingly written adventure story about the German naturalist Alexander von Humboldt and his explorations. The sections on Venezuela and especially the Orinoco are vivid and exciting.

Davis, Richard Harding. *Three Gringos in Venezuela and Central America*. New York: Harper & Brothers, 1896. 281 pp. Davis, then thirty-two, traveled with two young well-to-do friends, Lloyd Griscom and Henry Somers Somerset, and Charlwood, "young Somerset's servant," first to Belize, then Puerto Barrios, Guatemala, then on a memorable mule ride (the only way to get there) from San Pedro Sula to Tegucigalpa, and finally to Caracas, which after these primitive places looked like "the Paris of South America." His comments on all these places are very superficial, mostly opportunities for the glamorous journalist to pose in exotic places, but some of the descriptions of Caracas are useful.

Ralegh, Sir Walter. *The Discovery of the Large, Rich, and Bewtiful Empire of Guiana. . . .* London: The Hakluyt Society, 1848. Reprinted from the edition of 1596, edited and with copious explanatory notes and a biographical memoir by Sir Robert H. Schomburgk, Ph.D. The delight of this edition is that the German naturalist and explorer Schomburgk (exploring Guiana for the British) is as colorful and engaging as Ralegh.

Robertson, Ruth. *Churún Merú—The Tallest Angel: Of Jungles and Other Journeys.* Ardmore, PA: Whitmore Publishing Company, 1975. 345 pp. An exciting adventure story that not only tells about Angel Falls but gives a vivid picture of what life was like in Caracas in the 1940's for an adventurous American woman.

Chapter III

Fox, Geoffrey. "Honor, Shame, and Women's Liberation in Cuba." In Ann Pescatello, ed., *Female and Male in Latin America: Essays*. Univ. of Pittsburgh Press, 1973, pp. 273–290. Although focusing on another country, presents a detailed description of Hispanic traditions that are just as important in modern Venezuela.

Newson, Linda A. "Indian Population Patterns in Colonial Spanish America." *Latin American Research Review*, Vol. XX (1985) No. 3, pp. 41–74.

O'Hanlon, Redmond. "Amazon Adventure." *Granta* Vol. 20 (Winter 1986), pp. 15–54. Includes an account of the author's *yoppo* trip in the company of a Yanomami headman.

Rouse, Irving. *Venezuelan Archeology*. New Haven: Yale Univ. Press, 1963. 179 pp. Discusses the cultures that were present before the Europeans arrived.

Wilbert, Johannes. *Survivors of Eldorado: Four Indian Cultures of South America*. New York: Praeger, 1972. 212 pp. Summarizes anthropological findings on the Yanomami, Makaratire, Warao, and Goajiro peoples of Venezuela, with several black-and-white photographs of all four.

Chapter IV

Lombardi, John V. *Venezuela: The Search for Order, The Dream of Progress*. New York: Oxford Univ. Press, 1982. 348 pp. The best short history in English.

Rudolph, James. Chapter 1 in *Venezuela: A Country Study*. Richard Haggerty, ed. Washington: U.S.G.P.O. Takes us through the 1983 election.

Von Hagen, Victor Wolfgang. *The Germanic People in America*. Norman, OK: Univ. of Oklahoma Press, 1976. 403 pp. Chapter IV, "The Golden Man," gives a fascinating and detailed account of how the House of Welser got involved in Venezuela and of the Welser employees' mad searches for El Dorado. There are also somewhat skimpier treatments of Humboldt's travels and of the Germans who served in Bolívar's armies.

Chapter V

Masur, Gerhard. *Simon Bolivar*. Albuquerque: Univ. of New Mexico Press, 1969. 572 pp. This is still the best available biography in English.

Chapter VI

Matthews, Robert P. *Rural Outlaws in 19th Century Venezuela: Antecedent to the Federalist War*. New York Univ., Ibero-American Language and Area Center, Occasional Papers No. 4, 1973. A very short but colorful study of early *llaneros*.

Hendrickson, Embert J. "Gunboats, Dependency, and Oil: Issues in United States–Venezuelan Relations." *Latin American Research Review*, Vol. XX (1985), No. 2, pp. 262–67. Review essay.

Ybarra, T. R. *The Passionate Warrior: Simón Bolívar.* New York: Ives Washburn, Inc., 1929, 1942.

————. *Young Man of Caracas.* New York: Ives Washburn, 1942. 342 pp. The son of General Alejandro Ybarra, a Liberal and an intermittently important figure in Caracas politics, and of Massachusetts-reared Nelly Russell, recalls revolutions, folkways, and personalities of his adolescence in the Caracas of the 1890's.

Chapter VII

Ellner, Steve. *Venezuela's Movimiento al Socialismo: From Guerrilla Defeat to Innovative Politics*. Durham, NC: Duke Univ. Press, 1988. 262 pp. A thorough study of the origins and development of Venezuela's most important leftist party, which grew out of the *guerrilla* movement of the 1960's.

Karl, Terry Lynn. "Petroleum and Political Pacts: The Transition to Democracy in Venezuela." *Latin American Research Review*, Vol. XXII (1987), No. 1, pp. 63–94. An influential interpretation of the ways in which Acción Democrática and COPEI have split up power and privileges to keep other political groups out.

Matthews, Robert. "Oil on Troubled Waters: Venezuelan Policy in the Caribbean." *NACLA* [North American Committee on Latin America] *Report on the Americas*, Vol. XVIII (1984), No. 4 (July/August), pp. 23–43. Historical background from 1959 on, useful "mini facts" page (with map) p. 25.

Rourke, Thomas. *Gómez: Tyrant of the Andes*. New York: William Morrow, 1936. 320 pp. This biography of Juan Vicente Gómez, written right after his death when the memory of his regime was most vivid, is filled with details, interviews, and photographs. As the title suggests, it is not unbiased.

Salazar-Carrillo, Jorge. "Industrialization and Development in Venezuela." *Latin American Research Review*, Vol. XXI (1986), No. 3, pp. 257–266. Review essay.

Chapter VIII

Latin American Literature in the 20th Century. New York: Ungar, 1986. The chapter on Venezuelan literature, pp. 259–268, has capsule descriptions of major twentieth-century authors, with more extended discussions of Rómulo Gallegos and Arturo Uslar Pietri. However, it is badly outdated—no work published after 1955 is even mentioned.

Margolies, Luise. "The Canonization of a Venezuelan Folk Saint: The Case of José Gregorio Hernández." *Journal of Latin American Lore*, Vol. 14 (1988), No. 1, pp. 93–110. One of the few studies available in English discusses the miracles that have been attributed to Dr. Hernández since his death and includes a bibliography of relevant articles and books, mostly in Spanish.

Pollak-Eltz, Angelina. *María Lionza, mito y culto venezolano*. Caracas: Universidad Católica Andrés Bello, 1985. 139 pp. This is the most thorough and objective account of the very popular cult of María Lionza; there is almost nothing available on the subject in English. Pollak-Eltz analyzes the contradictions and the illogical character of these magical beliefs while acknowledging their power to produce apparent cures (some of which she has witnessed) of both physical and psychological complaints.

Chapter IX

Kurusa. *La calle es libre*. Caracas: Ediciones Ekare—Banco del Libro, 1986, first edition 1981. Drawings by Monika Doppert. This is based on the true story of a group of Caracas children who tried, unsuccessfully, to have a park built in their *barrio*. In Spanish, but so beautifully and vividly illustrated that one can get a good feel of *barrio* life even without the text.

Chapter X

Financial Times. Survey of Venezuela, February 21, 1990. Contains very informative articles on economic conditions and current political and social problems.

Discography

Listings below indicate label, whether recording is CD (compact disc) or LP, and order number.

Folk Music

Ballet Folklórico—Danzas Venezuela. Monitor (LP) MFS-499

Soledad Bravo is a guitarist and singer with a rich, emotive voice. She has made many recordings of traditional Venezuelan songs of the countryside, among them:
Cantares de Venezuela. Inter-American (LP) OAS-010
Cantos de Venezuela. Polydor (LP) 30 156
Flor de Cacao. Gamma (LP) GX 01-1188. The title song is especially lovely.

The Music of Venezuela. High Water (LP) LP-1013. This is a sampler of traditional music, with songs by many different artists and groups.

Cándido Herrera y su Conjunto. *Folklore de Venezuela.* Corona (CD) C.D.-07. Includes music from all regions, including the Andes, Zulia, the Llanos, etc.

Juan Vicente Torrealba y su Conjunto. *Concierto en la* Llanura. Gilmar (CD) C.D.G. 02

Mario Guacarán. *Venezuela—Arpa Llanera.* A.S.P.I.C. (CD) x55507; with commentary in English and French. This and the preceding entry are both instrumentals, featuring the traditional Venezuelan harp of the Llanos, a large, mellow wooden instrument with gut strings.

Los Machucambos Sing the Music of Venezuela. London International (LP) SW 99434. This is an old record that may be hard to find but is worth the effort. It contains twelve traditional songs, mostly from the Llanos and many featuring harp, maracas, and *cuatro*, sung by one woman and three or four men. The rendition of "Alma Llanera" is inspired.

Popular and Rock

Franco de Vita. *Extranjero.* CBS Discos International (CD) CD-80528

Yordano. *Finales de Siglo.* SONO (CD) SO-1449. Yordano and de Vita are two of Venezuela's most popular male singers, and their recordings are widely available in the United States. If you are in a Latin American neighborhood, you may also be able to find recordings by other Venezuelan pop singers, such as Ricardo Montaner, José Luis Rodríguez ("El Puma"), and the popular *telenovela* star Carlos Matta.

Classical

Alirio Díaz is an internationally acclaimed classical guitarist. For Vanguard he has recorded music of Vivaldi (LP and CD) HM32 and of Boccherini (LP and CD) 291.

Index

Numbers in *italics* refer to illustrations.

Guzmán Blanco, Antonio, 6, 7, 99–105, *103*, 150

Haiti, 39, 77
hammock weaving, *47*
headless men, legend of, 53, 55
Hernández, José Gregorio, 135, *136*
Herrera Campins, Luis, 102, 127, 171
higher education, 150–51
highways, 120, 158–59
Hispaniola, 39
History of New Granada (Rodríguez Freyle), 54
honor, Spanish attitudes, 46–48
horses and horse-racing, 25, 39, 152–54
housing project, *161*
howler monkeys, 15, 29
Hudson, W. H., 29
Humboldt, Alexander von, 15, 16, 27, 29
Humboldt, Hotel, 120–21
Humboldt mountain, 24
hunter-gatherer groups, 37, 40–41
Hutten, Philipp von, 53

igneous rocks, 12
IMF (International Monetary Fund), 167, 168, 173
immigrants, 49
income, per-capita, 5
independence from Spain, 1, 65–66
  struggle for, 68–89
Indians (indigenous peoples), 36–42, *38*, *39*, 43, *51*, 52, *52*, 57, 66, *133*, 134, 135
  houses, *5*, 39
  and independence, 76
industrialization, 128
  oil boom and, 113

intermarriage, blacks and Indians, 44
iron, 29
Italian immigrants, 49

James I, King of England, 30
jasper, 3, 30
juntas, 65–67, 117–22

Kennedy, John F., *123*

labor movement, 105
La Guaira, 17, 21, 57, 58, *62*
languages, indigenous, 37
Lara, 36, 39, 43
Larrazábal, Wolfgang, 121–22
Law of Lashes, 96
Legalist Revolution, 105
Léon, Juan Francisco de, 62–63
Leoni, Raúl, 126
Liberal Oligarchy, 97–98
Liberal Restoration Revolution, 105
Liberator. *See* Bolívar
Liendo, Eduardo, 142
literacy rate, 3, 150
literature, 137–42
llaneros (plainsmen), 24, 71–74, *73*, 75, 80, 92, 96
  politics of, 97–98
llanos, 11, 24–26, 72–73, 92, 95, *95*
  formation of, 17
  rainfall, 12
  revolutionary war, 80
Llovera Páez, Luis Felipe, 117–18
López Contreras, Eleazar, 115–16, 117
Lusinchi, Jaime, 129, 171, 175

MacGregor, Gregor, 79
machismo, Spanish, 46–48

transportation, 21, 106, 149, 158–59
  highways, 120
  Orinoco River, 27–28
  railroads, 21, 104
  subway, 156, *157*
Trinidad, 21
Trujillo (town), 56
Trujillo, Rafael Leonidas, 122
turpial (national bird), 2

Unare River, 21
unions, 113, 126
United States, 109, 122, 155
  Pérez and, 171, 173
  trade with, 113, 126
urbanization, 3, 113
URD (Democratic Republican Union),
  118, 119, 121, 122, 127
Uslar-Gleichen, Baron Johannes von,
  78
Uslar Pietri, Arturo, 139

Valencia, 56, 149
Vallenilla Lanz, Laureano, 102
Vargas, José María, 93
Venezuela, Gulf of, 17
Venezuela heróica (Blanco), 138

Vespucci, Amerigo, 19, 51
Villalba, Jóvito, 118, 119
Villanueva, Carlos Raúl, 156

Waldseemüller, Martin, 51
War of independence, Bolívar and,
  70–71
Washington Protocol, 109
waterfall, 12–13
Welser (German trading company), 53
wheat-flour mill, *60*
whites, 36
  and independence, 66, 76
wildlife, 1, 13, 14–16, 29
women, 46–48, 53, 55
  Bolívar and, 87
  Gómez and, 111
  warriors, 55–56
work, Spanish attitudes to, 46

Yanomami, 40–41
Ybarra, T. R., 101, 105, 109
  Young Man of Caracas, 106–7

zambos, 44
Zamora, Ezequiel, 97, 99

YA
987
Fox, Geoffrey.
The land and people of Venezuela.